Powerful Medical Device Sales Guidebook

By Daniel Farb, M.D., Bruce Gordon, Susan Postnikoff, and Cynthia Drake, RN

Please send any correspondence regarding permissions to:
UniversityOfHealthCare
419 N. Larchmont Blvd., #323
Los Angeles, CA 90004

Powerful Medical Device Sales Guidebook

ISBN: 1594912645

Library of Congress Catalog Number: 2005925203

UniversityOfHealthCare website: www.uohc.com

Contents

Introduction

This book is a text-only version of our acclaimed CD products on medical device and pharmaceutical sales. We have made it for those who prefer books. However, we have tried to retain the flavor of the CD approach with some use of review questions and a conversational tone.

We recommend that, if you have training needs or need to document your mastery of this material, you obtain the CD also. Also, the whole interview section on customer management, available only in the CD, works best in a medium where tone and body language come across.

Our goal is to help you increase your sales by being a helpful colleague to the professionals you work with and by serving the patients appropriately. That is the only basis for solid long-term sales.

About the Authors

M. Daniel Farb, CEO of UniversityOfHealthCare and UniversityOfBusiness, is a leader in the field of interactive management and healthcare e-learning. He received a BA in English Literature from Yale (where he set an academic record and studied with writers like Robert Penn Warren), an M.D. from Boston University, a degree in Executive Management from the Anderson School of Business at UCLA, and is currently working on a degree at UCLA in International Trade. He is a practicing ophthalmologist. He also has received two patents in ophthalmology and is working on others, has worked with the World Health Organization in Geneva and the National Institutes of Health in Washington, D.C. He has written scientific and popular articles, and has worked as a newspaper reporter. He helped Dr. Robbins edit one of the editions of Robbins' "Pathology" textbook for readability. He wrote an article on humor for the Massachusetts Review. He has experience in theater and television, including acting, directing, and stage-managing. He has programmed his own patient records database. He has written and edited hundreds of e-learning courses.

Dr. Farb is a member of the American Academy of Ophthalmology, the Union of American Physicians and Dentists, the AOJS, the American Association of Physicians and Surgeons, the ASTD (American Society for Training and Development), the E-Learning Forum, the Southern California Biomedical Council, the PDA (Parenteral Drug Association), and the Medical Marketing Association.

BRUCE GORDON is the Creative Director for UniversityOfHealthCare. After receiving a BA in Economics from UCLA, he began a freelance writing career that included technical writing (such as a manual for Princess Cruise Lines), stand-up comedy routines for nationally known comedians, and screenplay writing. He has done production support work with famous Hollywood personalities on such well-known productions as Aaron Spelling's "Dynasty" and "Love Boat" TV shows. An audio-visual software specialist, he is a versatile artist, with published works in a variety of media, including music, motion graphics, and digital video short film.

SUSAN POSTNIKOFF worked as a Sales Representative and Medical Distributor for more than 12 years. Susan successfully created and managed a medical distribution company, and was particularly successful at assessing the value and potential of new technologies in the medical device industry. As Sales Representative and Territory Manager for Danek (now known as Medtronic Sofamor Danek), Susan produced consecutive sales increases of **109%, 44%, and 128%** in the same geographical area, increasing the market share from approximately 22% to well over 60%. As a distributor, Susan was able to recognize the specific needs of customers as unique and different entities, and to formulate plans to meet those needs. In order to fulfill her plans, she was successful in gaining the cooperation of medical device companies to deliver the resources required to produce exceptional results.
Susan credits her sales success to her ability and willingness to listen for her customer's needs, preferences and way of doing business, and strategizing to address those; rather than finding ways to make the customer fit into her existing strategies. Susan has the ability to foster relationships with customers over time that result in loyalty and trust, and her customers have attested to her business ethics since her first day in the industry. During her sales career, she was called on by her employers, and also by her peers, to advise and lecture on how to succeed as a sales representative in the hospital setting. Susan also has experience organizing and leading training sessions for nurses, medical

students, residents, physical therapists, chiropractors and various hospital staff members. She has received excellent reviews for her part as an organizer and leader of such training. Susan has been particularly successful in developing partnership relationships with customers in the hospitals that she has worked with, and is now consulting with some of those customers to develop hospital-specific policies and procedures and training requirements for Industry Representatives.

CYNTHIA DRAKE received her MBA from the University of Houston (Texas) and has a Diploma in Nursing from Brackenridge Hospital in Austin (Texas). She has experience working with startup and development stage medical device and pharmaceutical firms. Cynthia has worked as a journalist, columnist, and consultant to the medical device industry, and has been called upon as an expert witness.
Cynthia has authored several articles regarding the market for various minimally invasive surgical procedures, and has been called upon as a consultant to write over 100 customized strategic marketing reports, market research reports and traditional marketing and business plans for medical device manufacturers. As a marketing executive with a variety of medical equipment and device manufacturers, Cynthia has coordinated distribution agreements and product launches and has supervised and trained product managers around the world. Cynthia has produced exceptional sales results for both new product launches, and existing product lines as a result of implementing her marketing plans.
Cynthia's extensive hospital experience includes having served as the O.R. Supervisor at the Park Plaza Hospital, and as the Director of Operating Rooms at St. Luke's-Texas Children's-Texas Heart Institute.

Powerful Medical Device Sales

1. Introduction

Goals of the course:

As a result of this course, healthcare providers and medical manufacturers will significantly reduce the liability imposed upon them by medical sales representatives working in the hospital, operating room (O.R.) and medical office setting. This will be accomplished via training in areas including – but not limited to – the HIPAA Privacy Rule, sales and marketing Code of Conduct, infection control and bloodborne pathogens, O.R. protocol, hospital policies and procedures for vendors, tissue handling guidelines and standards, and effective communication.

The medical manufacturers and sales representatives will learn that the best way to make great sales is by appropriate behavior and professional attitudes based on communication skills in a consultative relationship that helps the providers obtain the best treatment for their patients.

This course is primarily for medical devices; UniversityOfHealthCare has a separate course for pharmaceutical representatives called Powerful Pharmaceutical Sales. Since many manufacturers also sell pharmaceuticals, much of that information is included here. However, this course, Powerful Medical Device Sales, has much additional material specific to medical devices.

Course Content

Medical sales representatives will be trained on:

- HIPAA Implications for Industry Representatives

- Infection Control and Blood Borne Pathogens
- Ethical Sales/Code of Conduct
- O.R. Protocol
- Procedures for Loaned Instrumentation and Equipment
- Sexual Harassment
- Effective Communication and Questioning Styles
- Customer Management Cycle
- Hospital policies and procedures, including non-compliance

This program is designed to give the sales professional a comprehensive understanding of selling in the institutional setting and in the provider's office.

This course will complement the product training and sales skills already possessed by the salesperson, and will provide the necessary information to build confident partnerships with institutional operating rooms and pharmacies. The result will be long-term exceptional sales results through investigational and consultative selling.

2. Hospitals and the Medical Manufacturing Industry

Hospitals are organized in a variety of ways. They serve different sections of the population in different ways. A hospital may be part of a much larger enterprise or system. Such systems may include outpatient facilities, medical schools, nursing schools and doctors' offices. Hospitals are classified as either for-profit or not-for-profit.

The following are various hospital types, with respect to populations treated, and some additional classifications that you will typically encounter as a hospital sales representative. A brief description is given for each.

--General Medical Surgical

This is the most common hospital type, has a multitude of departments, and treats virtually all diseases and conditions. Some may become known for treating specific conditions via word of mouth or through advertising.

--Specialty

Specialty hospitals treat special populations such as women or children, or may specialize in certain conditions such as cancer or heart disease (i.e., Arizona Heart Hospital).

--Psychiatric

These treat the mentally ill, who are typically medically normal individuals.

--Rehabilitation and Chronic Disease

Patients here generally live in the hospital or are outpatients for extended periods of time as a result of trauma or disease that requires extended rehabilitation to be able to function independently.

--Long Term Acute Care

When a patient requires care for a period exceeding the hospital stay that is allowed by the insurer, that patient is transferred to a less acute, but skilled facility. May be called a SNF (skilled nursing facility).

--Government or Military

Most military bases have at least a small hospital to serve the military and their families. Additionally, there are very large tertiary care centers such as Balboa Medical Center (San Diego) where all forms of healthcare are available The Veterans' Administration (VA) supports at least 23 large hospitals in the US.

--Profit vs. Not-for-Profit

Profit-based hospitals tend to be privately owned and operated by an individual or corporation. Not-for-profit hospitals are most often owned by a non-profit organization such as a church, charitable organization, or government.

--Academic vs. Non-teaching

Academic or teaching hospitals are affiliated with a university or college, and include staff and student or resident physicians, surgeons, and nurses.

--Community-based vs. Tertiary

Community-based hospitals are usually general medical and surgical centers and sometimes serve as teaching hospitals as well. Tertiary hospitals provide highly specialized services for severe illness and conditions, and may have specialty units such as coronary or neonatal intensive care units, and are usually teaching hospitals.

Additionally, hospitals or care units can be stratified by the intensity level of nursing care needed. The most demanding nursing care is in the hospital in its specialized departments. Next comes long-term acute care centers. Then patients may be admitted to Skilled Nursing Facilities (SNFs) and at the end of the range is the Nursing Home.

Effect of Hospital Type on the Sales Process

As you plan your selling strategy at a particular account it will be important to note the type of hospital you are working with. Government hospitals may be focused on cost savings. Academic Hospitals will be more likely to try out new treatments, and your strategy here might include working with your company to utilize the account for clinical trials and other research projects. Profit-oriented hospitals need to strike a balance between marketability and profitability. Non-profit hospitals may need to attract the press by offering new therapies, in order to attract funding. Community-based hospitals may be more likely to stick with known and trusted therapies and treatments in order to maintain consistent outcomes. There may be particular physicians within a facility that want notoriety for academic pursuits, and there may be those who want to be known for their conservatism. Ask your customers what is important to them – their answers may surprise you!

Hospital Structure and Decision Making Process

Hospitals are organized by departments, most often managed by Department Directors. In very large healthcare enterprises the department managers may hold titles similar to those in the business world, i.e., Vice-President. There will be a Director of Pharmacy, a Director of Nursing Services, Director of Materials Management (purchasing), etc. The Credentials Committee regulates physicians working in a hospital environment. This committee decides which physician can work in the institution and awards credentials for the specialty practice he/she will perform. The Credentials Committee can both award and revoke privileges.

Physicians, and in some instances Nurse Practitioners (a specially educated and licensed category of registered nurses), are allowed by law to prescribe medicines. They have input, but not total control, over the list of medicines to be used in any given hospital environment. They can request that a new drug be made available, but either the Credentialing Committee or Pharmacy and Therapeutics Committee has the final say for which drugs are added or deleted from the formulary.

Decisions about which products or drugs to purchase are often a function of a committee or team including representatives from affected departments within the institution.

Medicines are purchased either directly by the Pharmacy Department's buyer or through the hospital-wide purchasing department. Departments such as Respiratory Therapy may use medications that are delivered directly to the department; however, the medications are always purchased by the Pharmacy. The inventory held in the pharmacy is determined by the formulary, and by the level of dcmand for the individual medication.

Physicians and nurse practitioners (in some states) are the only people who can write a prescription for a drug. The prescription is written on the patient's chart. Nurses are responsible for transmitting that physician order to the pharmacy where a pharmacist dispenses the requested medicine to the nursing unit. A licensed vocational (or practical) nurse or a registered nurse is authorized to dispense the medication as described in the physician's order.

When drugs are dispensed for an individual patient, most nursing services request the drugs be available in unit doses. These are packages or vials containing only enough medicine for one dose for the individual patient.

Review Question: The following healthcare professionals may prescribe medication for a patient (choose the BEST answer):
a) Physician
b) Registered nurse
c) Pharmacist
d) Nurse Practitioner
e) A and C
f) A and D
Answer: f

Hospital Departments

Most hospitals have a variety of departments located conveniently for the department's function. Standard departments are described below. The most important departments for a pharmaceutical representative are the Hospital Pharmacy and the Medical Staff. Those will be treated individually at some depth. Here we describe other departments the medical device or pharmaceutical representative needs to know about.

--Emergency Room (ER)

The ER accepts and treats patients who require immediate medical attention. The TV show with this name shows exactly how a large ER functions. Patients may present with a range of conditions including fractured wrists, lawnmower-amputated toes, heart attacks, and major trauma (to list only a few!). In the case of a major terrorist action all injured would be taken to emergency rooms. There the nursing and physician staff perform triage—they decide which patients to treat first and which ones to leave for later. Physicians who specialize in ER duty do not usually have regular patients or offices. The ER is their office. The ER physician may call upon specialists to provide additional consultations. Any area of specialty may be called upon from Orthopedic Surgery to Psychiatry. Additionally, the ER will interact with various labs and radiology departments. A fracture room or cast room is generally located in or ncar emergency in order to cast or splint injuries.

--Pediatrics

This is a floor or a wing of the institution where patients from newborn to 16 years of age are admitted. Some hospitals specialize in pediatrics, taking no adults whatsoever.

As examples: Children's Hospital of San Diego (San Diego, CA) and Texas Children's Hospital (Houston, Texas).

--Obstetrics and gynecology (OB-GYN)

This area of the hospital is located close to Labor and Delivery. A portion of the number of beds on the unit is dedicated to women with surgical or medical needs. The majority of the beds are for mothers who have recently delivered.

--Labor and Delivery

This is a specialized unit of the hospital. There are several very small rooms where the mother undergoes the labor experience. From the labor room when the baby is about ready to be born, the mother is moved into an operating room called the Delivery Room. After delivering the child, mothers are usually transferred to an OB-GYN unit.

--Nursery

As the new mother is being moved to her room on the OB-GYN unit, the newborn child is usually taken to the Nursery. Here well babies are cared for until a day or so later when mother and baby go home. Some mothers prefer to keep their newborn with them at all times.

--Neonatal Intensive Care Unit (NICU)

When babies are born prematurely or with life-threatening congenital abnormalities, they are transferred to the NICU. Here, specially trained nurses and physicians care for the babies. Specialized physicians on this service are known as neonatologists.

--Intensive Care Unit (ICU)

The intensive care unit is often built in the round. That is, the nursing station may be in the center of a large area while the patients' rooms form the outer ring of the circle. In this arrangement, the nursing personnel can more easily monitor all activity in their unit. Patients admitted to ICU may have recently had a heart attack, may have been severely injured in an auto accident, or may have just undergone very major surgery. Patients admitted to the ICU require top level nursing care. The ratio of nurses to patients is often no more than 1:2. Physicians who specialize in the ICU are called intensivists.

They work only in the intensive care units of the hospital. Some hospitals have a separate cardiac ICU (CICU).

--Surgery Department

The surgery department consists of a preoperative area, an operative area and a postoperative area. Nursing personnel in this environment are known as perioperative nurses. Patients scheduled for surgery are brought from their rooms to the pre-op area. Here a nurse starts the intravenous line and takes a short history from the patient. The anesthesiologist may prescribe medication. After the pre-op meds are given, the patient is taken to the assigned OR and the surgical team performs the requested surgery. The surgical team includes the surgeon, the anesthesiologist, the circulating nurse and a scrub nurse. Once the surgery is complete the patient is moved into the PACU (post-anesthesia care unit). All varieties of surgery may be performed in an OR suite. In larger hospitals there may be specific rooms designated (reserved) for a high volume subspecialty. This could be neurosurgery, cardiovascular surgery, urology, or others.

--The PACUs

These are immediately approximate to the OR, and they accept patients directly from their surgery. The PACU may also be referred to as the recovery room. These patients are in varying states of alertness as the anesthesia is reversed. Nurses in this area monitor the patients as they become fully awake. Once the patient is fully alert, he is moved back to his room on the appropriate hospital ward (each area of specialization--orthopedics, ob-gyn, etc.-- generally has its own ward with patient rooms and a nursing station).

--Respiratory Therapy Department

Respiratory therapists staff this section of the hospital. These technically trained individuals administer breathing procedures as prescribed by physicians. A wide variety of breathing machines resides in this department. Some assist patients with chronic obstructive pulmonary disease (COPD) while others keep breathing for patients when they cannot do so for themselves. Certain medications may be used in the respiratory therapy department, and thus there may be a need for the pharmaceutical representative to call on personnel in this department, or provide information on specific medications to this department.

--Radiology

This is the department of the hospital where X-rays are done. It is a diagnostic unit and may also offer MRI (magnetic resonance imaging), CT (computed tomography), and other very sophisticated diagnostic techniques.

Radiotherapy may be a subsection of the radiology department. One technique involves IMRT (intensity modulated radio therapy). Radiologists with special skills, oncologists, and medical physicists work in this arena.

--Interventional Radiology

This department is another subset of the radiology area. These specialists are radiologists with more training. They treat a variety of diseases using minimally invasive techniques—percutaneous procedures. They are called percutaneous, because, as opposed to regular surgery, the procedures are done through the skin using a needle stick or a small incision into a vessel. Special wires, baskets, and probes have been designed for use inside blood vessels, bladder, ureter, and kidney. The interventional radiologist performs these procedures using fluoroscopy—an active X-ray type device—as his image-producing medium.

--Cardiac Services and Interventional Cardiology

The department of cardiology may have associated with it a variety of labs and diagnostic services including a Stress Test Laboratory and an Interventional Cardiology Laboratory. This department offers consultation, patient evaluation and diagnosis as well as treatment for a variety of cardiac-related disorders and diseases including arrhythmias and congestive heart failure. The interventional cardiologist may work either in a division of the Cardiology Department or the Radiology Department in different hospitals. Interventional Cardiologists perform a variety of minimally invasive procedures and often use fluoroscopy for imaging of their procedures. Wires, baskets, and other devices are used to reach different areas of the heart or major vessels. Coronary artery catheterization with ballooning and stenting is one of the most common procedures done by interventional cardiologists.

--Ancillary, Supporting Departments

The other departments in the hospital are non-clinical, that is, they don't care for patients. Instead, these departments support the clinical areas. These include housekeeping, laundry, cafeteria, security, purchasing, and administration.

Some institutions also offer a day surgery or outpatient surgery unit as part of their clinical service. Here simpler surgical procedures are performed. In these, the patient can be dismissed home within 23 hours. Examples of surgeries that might be performed in an outpatient surgicenter are arthroscopy of the knee or shoulder, operations on hands and feet, cataract surgery, and some types of back surgery.

The departments you call on will depend for the most part on your product. You will need to determine what departments, and whom within those departments you need to see. As you meet with the pharmacist and the physicians and specialists who will prescribe or use your product, you can ask who in each of the hospital's departments may impact upon the decision making process, and who may need information about your products. There also may be directors or managers from various departments who sit on committees involved in the decision making process such as the Credentialing Committee or Pharmacy and Therapeutics Committee.

3. The Medical Staff

Most physicians in the hospital are not employees. They are individual practitioners with their own patients and offices. Some physicians have specialized in only hospital care. These doctors are called hospitalists. They take care of patients only in the hospital, reporting back to the primary care physician in his office. Hospitalists may be paid by the institution, and others are paid by the primary care physician.

A particular hospital may choose to have a particular variety of specialists working with the institution. In the case of a specialized hospital, there may be only a few specializations, and related supporting departments. The hospital's credentialing committee decides the make-up of the medical staff. Usually one physician is given the title and responsibility of Chief of Staff. Also, one surgeon, regardless of specialization, may be named Chief of Surgery for the entire hospital. The chief of any specialty may be influential in getting the other specialists to agree to a certain product or protocol.

The following are several typical Specialist Clinics and/or Departments, each of which likely has a number of physicians, with one designated as Chief for each area of specialization. There will likely be nurses and other staff members working within each department to support the physicians. These specialized departments are very common in teaching hospitals, and as such will have residents and fellows training in each specialty or department. Within each specialty, the physicians may also each have chosen sub-specialties.
--Allergy-Immunology

Allergy-Immunology provides diagnosis and treatment of allergic conditions and immunologic disorders through medication, immunotherapy, and environmental control. The department will provide care for anaphylaxis, asthma and other allergic diseases, drug reactions, food allergies, occupational lung diseases and allergies, sinusitis, and urticaria, as well as for general allergic conditions.

--Anesthesia

The department of Anesthesia will provide a range of anesthesia services for inpatient and outpatient procedures. This may include outpatient preoperative assessments, inpatient preoperative assessments, acute and chronic pain management services and both pre- and postoperative critical care. Subspecialty areas may include of obstetrical, cardiac and transplant anesthesia, pain medicine, and critical care medicine. The pain medicine service performs interventional nerve blocks and may administer opioids via indwelling epidural catheters.

--Family Medicine

Some hospitals may have family medicine departments where General Practitioners specialize in family practice. These physicians offer primary care for adults and children. General Practitioners have a very difficult job in that they must know enough about all specialties and sub-specialties to know when and where to refer patients that need specific attention.

--Neurosciences

Stroke, epilepsy, acute back pain, movement disorders, and brain tumors such as acoustic neuroma and skull-based tumors are just a few of the serious, debilitating diseases and conditions of the spine and central nervous system that may be diagnosed and treated through the neurosciences department. Physicians within this department are usually neurosurgeons, however, the neurosurgeons may work in conjunction with orthopedic surgeons who specialize in spine, or with Ear, Nose, and Throat specialists who specialize in acoustic neuroma. Most neurosurgeons have a sub-specialty such as brain tumor, aneurysm, or spine surgery. Neurosurgeons may also hold regular outpatient clinics such as spinal cord injury clinics for a specialized patient population.

--Orthopedic Surgery

Orthopedic Surgeons may sub-specialize in tumor, degenerative hips and knees, sports medicine and soft tissue injury, or spine (to name a few). Most hospitals have fracture clinics near the ER department, and the orthopedic surgeons generally see patients in the fracture clinic at least once each week, in addition to seeing patients in the office and on the ward after surgery.

--Spine Surgery

Some hospitals have designated spine departments separate from neurosurgery or orthopedic surgery. Orthopedic surgeons or neurosurgeons that have chosen a sub-specialty in spine may work through this department. Some academic institutions offer residency programs in Neurosurgery, Orthopedic Surgery, and Spine Surgery as separate programs. As this format is quite new, the Spine Surgery Residents and Fellows are trained by a combination of neurosurgeons and orthopedic surgeons at this time.

--Ophthalmology

This department offers consultation, diagnostic evaluation, and treatment of diseases and disorders related to vision. The ophthalmologist may also perform surgery to treat diseases related to vision.

--Pulmonology

The Pulmonology Department provides consultative services for the diagnosis, evaluation, and management of diseases of the respiratory tract. Patients are seen for assessment of any pulmonary problem including asthma, cough, tuberculosis, COPD, atelectasis, airway lesions, chronic or recurrent pneumonia, and sleep apnea.

--Psychiatry

The Psychiatry department may include psychiatrists, psychiatric nurses, clinical social workers, and therapists. The department will help patients who may be at risk to themselves or others, or who may be unable to care for themselves due to the symptoms of their psychiatric condition. Psychiatry departments offer evaluation and treatment of conditions such as depression and anxiety disorders, chemical dependency, and other mental health problems.

--Neurology

The department of neurology offers comprehensive inpatient and outpatient services for the diagnosis and management of neurological disorders, including headache, stroke, epilepsy, Parkinson's disease and other movement disorders, multiple sclerosis, dementia, peripheral neuropathy, myasthenia gravis, myopathy, and other neuromuscular diseases.

--Urology

The Urology department will provide diagnosis and treatment of a multitude of disorders including prostate enlargement, urinary tract infection, sexually transmitted diseases, infertility, kidney blockage, urinary incontinence, erectile dysfunction, and related oncology.

<u>Review Question:</u> The following surgical specialty is most likely to treat a patient with a back pain (choose the BEST answer):

a) Neurosurgeon
b) Orthopedic Surgeon
c) General Surgeon
d) Spine Surgeon
e) A and b
f) B and d
g) A, b and d

<u>Answer:</u> g

4. The Hospital Pharmacy

The hospital pharmacy is heavily computerized and, as a result, most pharmacists use a computer in their daily work, primarily in the areas of dispensing prescriptions, stock control and information storage and retrieval.

For many pharmacists, the attraction of hospital pharmacy is the general contact with patients and other healthcare professionals when visiting patient areas or serving outpatient clinics. The pharmacist has many opportunities to work with doctors and nurses to encourage effective and economical drug treatment. As the expert on medicines within the healthcare team, the pharmacist is the person most aware of the adverse effects which a medicine or combination of medicines may produce and is therefore well placed to look for the symptoms of such drug reactions. They can also give advice on dosage; suggest the most appropriate form of medication (e.g. tablet, injection, ointment, or inhaler) and point out to the medical staff any likely reactions between medicines being administered and particular foods or between different medicines. The pharmacist can also give an informed opinion as to the advisability of giving a certain medicine to an individual patient, in the context of the patient's overall medical condition. For example, some types of medicine designed to reduce blood pressure may be dangerous to people with heart failure and certain medications are contraindicated for care of pregnant women or children.

To help the pharmacist and all the other members of the hospital and community healthcare team, a library of drug information is maintained by most main hospital pharmacy departments. Some institutions use nationwide pharmacy companies as an outsourced pharmacy department.

Review Question: In a large hospital, some pharmacists specialize in such areas as device information more than dealing directly with patients. True or false?
Answer: True

5. The Hospital-Based Pharmacist

The hospital pharmacist is very much a member of a team. They are members not only of the pharmacy department, but also of the hospital team, working to provide the best possible service for the patient. Hospital pharmacy can be subdivided into areas requiring a wide variety of specialist skills. For instance, although most medicinal products are now supplied by the pharmaceutical industry, a small range of specialist items are still produced either in batches or as one-off preparations by production pharmacists in the hospital, e.g., cancer treatments or special feeding solutions for injection. A few pharmacists specialize in the preparation of radioactive medicines for the diagnosis or treatment of disease. This sub-specialty is known as radiopharmacy.

A team of laboratory-based pharmacists, who ensure that materials and processes meet all required standards, supports production activities. This hospital pharmacy quality control service uses many analytical and pharmaceutical techniques for assessing both the preparations produced in the hospital and those purchased from the pharmaceutical industry.
Most pharmacists are employees of the hospital where they work. However, outsourced pharmacy departments will bring their own pharmacists.

Pharmacy Training

All pharmacists have earned at least a Bachelor of Sciences degree in Pharmacy. However, in July 1992, a majority of the nation's schools and colleges of pharmacy voted to move toward awarding the Doctor of Pharmacy (Pharm.D.) degree as the only professional degree in pharmacy. A Pharm.D. degree requires four years of professional study, following a minimum of two years of pre-pharmacy study, for a total of six academic years following high school. Including pre-pharmacy study, the minimum educational program for a BS in Pharmacy is five academic years.

A sound education in math and science is an essential part of preparation for the study of pharmacy; so pre-pharmacy students take courses in biology, chemistry, physics, and mathematics. Also, good written and verbal communication skills are important in both the study and practice of pharmacy, so would-be pharmacists study literature, history, government, and social studies to develop a strong background during their pre-professional schooling.

Professional courses, i.e., those taken in pharmacy school include:

- Pharmacognosy: the study of the biology and biochemistry of naturally occurring drug products, such as herbs and those derived from plants and animals.
- Pharmacology: the study of the action and uses of drugs.
- Pharmaceutical chemistry: the application of basic organic and inorganic chemistry to medicines
- Pharmaceutics: a broad range of subjects, including introductory pharmacy, pharmaceutical calculations, preparations, techniques, dispensing pharmacy, biopharmaceutics (the effects of the dosage form on a medication's therapeutic activity).
- Clinical pharmacy: the study of patient care with special emphasis on drug products. During part of this area of their

education, many pharmacy students actually have hands-on experience with patients in a variety of health care settings.

- Drug information: the study of how to convey information about drugs to patients and other health care professionals.
- Pharmacy administration: principles and practices of business and law as they apply to pharmacy practice.

After graduating from pharmacy school an increasing number of students are seeking residency training in pharmacy practice, which adds another year or so to their total education. Over three hundred pharmacy residency programs are offered in hospitals, community pharmacies, and some specialized facilities.

Hospital Formulary

Each hospital has a list of approved medicines. This list is called a Formulary. If a prescribed drug is not on this list, the pharmacy cannot fill the prescription. The Pharmacy and Therapeutics Committee controls the Formulary.

The Joint Commission on Accreditation of Healthcare Organizations (JCAHO) inspects hospitals. They must be approved by this organization in order to receive reimbursement for services provided from Medicare. Most private payers set the same or higher standards than JCAHO for reimbursement purposes.

JCAHO sets standards for hospitals and measures them against those standards on an annual or biannual inspection. One of the standards from JCAHO is that the institution has a committee to review drug use and abuse. This is often named the Pharmacy and Therapeutics Committee. Representatives from a number of the hospital departments may be members: i.e., nurses, physicians, pharmacists and buyers. The ranking pharmacist usually chairs this committee.

The Pharmacy and Therapeutics Committee is responsible for reviewing the use of drugs by physicians in the facility. In some instances physicians may be prescribing the wrong drug for the patient's condition or may be overusing antibiotics. This committee sits as a form of peer review. This committee may institute counseling of physicians and nurses.

The committee can also recommend adoption of "clinical pathways." These are set routines and procedures and drugs recommended by a peer institution or developed within the committee's institution. The clinical pathway is an algorithm guiding the healthcare team to perform the best care at the least cost with the desired quality outcome for the patient and cost savings for the institution.

The P&T committee can range from a large committee of up to 50 members including physicians, pharmacists, administrators, nurses, dieticians, therapists, and a variety of healthcare professionals representing the different departments within the hospital. In smaller hospitals, the committee may be very small with only a few members such as the pharmacist, a few physicians, and perhaps someone from nursing and/or administration.

Review Question: What do you suppose would happen if a patient admitted to hospital was on medication prior to being admitted that is not on the hospital's formulary? (Choose the MOST COMPLETE answer.)
a) The patient would provide his or her own medication
b) The hospital would immediately add that patient's medication to their formulary

c) The patient's medication would be changed or discontinued
d) A and C
e) B and C
Answer: d

Drug Delivery Systems

A drug delivery system is a delivery system in which a drug (one component of the system) is integrated with another chemical, a drug administration device, or a drug administration process to control the rate of drug release, the tissue site of drug release or both. A drug administration device is an apparatus that is used for introducing a drug to the body or controlling its rate of introduction. Drug delivery systems include, but are not limited to, osmotic pumps, thermal isolation, transdermal patches, liposomal encapsulation, iontophoreses, phonophoresis, magnetic migration, and implantation. Drug administration devices include (but are not limited to) mechanical (e.g., balloon-driver), gravity-driven, and electromechanical pumps.

Pharmacists bear a substantial responsibility for ensuring optimal clinical outcomes from drug therapy and are suited by education, training, clinical expertise, and practice activities to assume responsibility for the professional supervision of drug delivery systems and administration devices.

Current Issues for Hospital Pharmacists

The healthcare industry today is much more complex and diverse than it was even in the mid-1990s. The Hospital Pharmacist must understand and take positions on a variety of issues including: bar coding, continuing process improvement and health economics in general.

The Food and Drug Administration (FDA) announced in February 2004 its final rule requiring bar codes on all medication packages, a mandate that is expected to improve patient safety in the nation's hospitals significantly. According to Secretary of Health and Human Services Tommy G. Thompson and FDA Commissioner Mark B. McClellan, MD, PhD. the FDA would require bar codes to include the National Drug Code (NDC) number, a system that contains the drug name, dosage form and strength.

The rule does not require that bar codes include a medication's lot number and expiration date—elements which American Society of Hospital Pharmacists (ASHP) and other healthcare organizations have called for as critical to patient safety—The FDA has assured ASHP that it will encourage manufacturers to include this information.

Review Question: The bar codes must include the device name, dosage form, strength, and expiration date. True or false?
Answer: False. At this time inclusion of the expiration date is not mandatory.

AHSP is a founding member of the National Alliance for Healthcare Information Technology, which has called for the FDA to establish a 5-year phase-in period for including expiration date and lot number in the bar code. The ASHP has also called for bar codes to be placed on both the inner and outer wrap of all drug packages, including single-unit doses.

Most hospital departments are striving to control their processes and products through ongoing Quality Assurance (QA). Until the mid-1980s, QA was a term and a process native only to manufacturing. In the last decade hospitals have begun to recognize that they are businesses with profits and losses, products, processes and clients.

Continuing process improvement (CPI) is a form of QA. Some of the common terms used in CPI are:
--Processes: how work gets done, who does what and how technology is used. This will ultimately determine your organization's success.
--Best practices: a term often used by hospital departments. These are examples of how other institutions accomplish their mission best. Assessing their department compared to a Best Practice allows identification and measurement of potential gaps in practices compared to other institutions or to ASHP guidelines. Prioritizing system improvements based on gap size and importance is one way that managers can improve their departments.

When focusing on CPI, the pharmacist will set initiatives for the department. Examples of initiatives are:

- Be operationally excellent
- Implement better controls and processes
- Get more patient focused
- Drive revenue up and unnecessary costs out

Economics is increasingly being used to make health policy decisions and pharmacists need to understand thc basic concepts involved. Health economics can be seen as a tool to help prioritize healthcare interventions so that maximum health benefits are provided to the population within the resource constraints that exist. The key concept underlying health economics is that an effective healthcare intervention such as the prescribing of an appropriate drug can be recommended for patients who will benefit.

The following terms may be encountered in economic evaluations:

- Direct costs: costs directly associated with the healthcare intervention.
- Indirect costs: costs associated with reduced productivity due to illness, disability, and death. They are typically calculated from the gross earnings of those in employment.
- Intangible costs: psychological costs associated with illness or treatment.
- Opportunity cost: the consequences of choosing between two alternatives. They reflect the fact that choices have to be made between interventions or drugs because of the scarcity of resources.

Two types of economic evaluations useful for hospital pharmacists include cost-minimization analysis (where only the costs are compared, not the benefits) and cost-effectiveness analysis (where benefits are measured in life-years gained or quality of life scores). A third type is cost benefit analysis. Cost benefit is the most commonly used technique in healthcare economic decisions. The benefits in this technique are measured in monetary terms, and the final result is expressed as a net monetary gain (or loss) or as a cost-benefit ratio.

Currently many types of third-party payment systems are in use, including such diverse payment mechanisms as Medicare prospective pricing [e.g., diagnosis-related groups (DRGs)], capitated payments for health maintenance organizations and cost-based reimbursement for commercial third-party insurance. Each third-party payer may use different payment or reimbursement mechanisms and each hospital's reimbursement may vary by its location, its primary third-party payer and its case mix. Pharmacy managers must be cognizant of the types of compensation received by their individual hospitals and must structure their pharmaceutical services in a manner that permits identification and monitoring of costs versus benefits under each payment mechanism.

In the mid-1980s, hospitals charged insurers (or third party payers as these are now known) on a cost-plus basis. Items used to treat the patient were marked up some percentage from cost and then billed to the insurer. The insurer paid. Those days are gone. Most healthcare in the US today is delivered and charged for using either a prospective payment or a capitated payment. In these situations the insurer has reached agreement with the provider (whether physician or institution) on how much money will be paid for each patient with a defined disease or condition. Therefore, any new drug, device or supply has a wall of change refusal to breach. Since the provider has set revenue per patient regardless of how that diseased patient is treated, the emphasis is on constantly lowering costs while maintaining quality of care. Any new drug, device, or supply has to be no more expensive than the one it is to replace. The most desired outcome is to add new drugs or devices only when they perform the same service in a better way at a lower unit cost with the same or improved patient care outcomes.

For some time, pharmacies in organized healthcare settings have been moving from a product-centered structure to a more patient-oriented clinical practice. Clinical pharmacy services or patient-oriented pharmaceutical services are now a recognized and necessary component of healthcare. New trends in reimbursement, such as prospective payment and capital payments, provide different incentives for hospitals to manage product lines instead of patient services.

This means that the primary focus of institutional pharmacy practice is shifting from a system of drug distribution to one of drug use control, which includes both drug distribution, and provision of information. As these clinical services become part of third-party payer agreements pharmacists will be able to bill and be reimbursed for their time.

American Society of Health-System Pharmacists (ASHP) is a trade organization (www.ashp.org/acutecare) that represents 2500 members in its Section of Inpatient Care Practitioners. The major goals of this group is to support the professional development of its members, expand access to education, implement evidence-based practice guidelines, improve standards of practice and improve the quality of work life for the pharmacist.

ASHP, the parent organization, is a 30,000 member national professional association that represents pharmacists who practice in hospital, health maintenance organizations, long-term care facilities, home care and other components of healthcare systems. AHSP has a long history of medication-error prevention efforts. The organization notes that a pharmacist's mission is to help people make the best use of medicines.

6. Nursing Service

Either a Nursing Director or a Vice President of Nursing Service manages the nursing service department. This individual usually has a BS and often a Master's degree. Some Directors also have MBAs. All clinical nursing personnel report to this department manager. These positions include supervisory nurses, clinical educators, Registered Nurses, Licensed Vocational (or in some states Practical) Nurses (LVN) and nursing aides. Persons whose title includes Registered Nurse (RN) have a minimum of 3 and often 6 years of higher education. LVNs are trained in about 18 months and aides may have had no formal training. Pharmaceutical representatives have very little contact with nurses except to provide product education. The exception here is in states where Nurse Practitioners are authorized to prescribe medications. There may also be nursing staff represented on the Pharmacy and Therapeutics Committee, and as such are important contacts for the pharmaceutical representative.

Device representatives may have more contact with nurses who manage devices used in nursing or supplies and equipment for the operating room.

Nurses read doctor's orders and turn those into a request for pharmacy to provide the right medication in the right dose at the right time. Only physicians, RNs, and LVNs are licensed to dispense/administer medications to patients.

In most instances the relationship between a nurse and a pharmacist is collegial. They are each part of a team striving toward the same outcome; quality patient care. Similarly one can help educate the other by sharing how drugs can be dispensed more easily or identified in a safer way. Both individuals want to prevent medication errors.

Review Question: LVNs are allowed to prescribe medications in certain states. True or false?
Answer: False. Nurse practitioners can sometimes prescribe.

Here is a scenario of a sales rep not understanding the nurse's relationship with doctors and the hospital pharmacy.
Rep: Hi, Nurse Jenkins, I thought I was going to see Dr. Smith today.

Nurse: Well, he asked me to see you, because, as you may know, we make both prescribe medications and we make our decisions together.
Rep: Well, usually I just see doctors.
Nurse: Oh... •

7. Typical Policies and Procedures for Hospital Vendors

Each hospital you may visit will have its own set of policies and procedures that representatives will be expected to know and adhere to. The following are common or typical policies and procedures you are likely to encounter.

--Appointments are Mandatory

Appointments are usually required in order for a representative to be allowed to enter a hospital. When you are visiting a hospital for the first time, you will need to contact the Pharmacy Department or Materials Management Department ahead of time, and ask for the appropriate protocol for requesting appointments and signing in. You will likely be directed either to Materials Management or Security to sign in.

<u>Review Question:</u> You are running 5 minutes late for an appointment with the hospital pharmacist. What do you do? (Choose the best answer.)

a) Sign-in after your appointment, so that you will be on time.
b) Call the pharmacist prior to your appointment and inform her you are running late.
c) Park in a reserved parking space closer to the door to save time.
d) Just get there as fast as possible, as 5 minutes likely won't be noticed.

<u>Answer:</u> b

--Vendor Parking

At most hospitals, representatives must park in visitor parking. Do NOT park in spaces designated for emergency vehicles, staff, clergy, MRI patients, or disabled persons. Certain hospitals may specify vendor parking and/or make allowances for representatives to utilize the receiving area to drop of equipment. Always request permission prior to utilizing the receiving dock or other loading or unloading areas. If you are given permission to use a patient loading area, ensure that you are not blocking any wheel chair access ramps or entrances.

--TB Testing & Illness

A recent negative TB Test result is typically required for all representatives entering an operating room or procedure room and may be required for any representative entering the hospital for any purpose. All representatives prior to entering the operating room - for their own safety, should have Hepatitis B vaccination. Representatives who are ill will not be permitted to enter the operating room or procedure rooms, ICU, or other patient treatment areas, and preferably should not enter the facility at all as per the following:

- Vendors must be free of infectious diseases and must not have been exposed to any communicable disease within the previous ten day.
- Representatives with viral or bacterial infections that may be transmitted by airborne transmission or by droplet transmission will not bc permitted in the surgical suite, and preferably should not enter the facility – this includes but is not limited to influenza, strep throat, and meningitis.

If you have a positive reaction to the tuberculosis skin test, it usually means that you have been exposed to the bacteria, but there is a better than 90% chance that your body's immune system has suppressed the infection. When your skin test is found to be newly positive, you will have a chest radiograph to make sure that you don't have an active infection. If your chest radiograph is negative and your skin test reaction is recent, you may be given an anti-tuberculosis medicine for 6 to 12 months. This medicine is used to prevent any activation of the infection in the future, but you are not infectious to others.

If you have a positive skin test and an abnormal chest radiograph or symptoms of tuberculosis, you'll be treated for active disease. When you're diagnosed with active disease, you're infectious to others. You may be treated with 3 or 4 medicines for 9 to 12 months. You'll need to take precautions with your family, and you'll be kept out of work until you're no longer infectious. Active tuberculosis is much less common than a tuberculosis infection your immune system can suppress on its own.

Once you have had a positive skin test, you shouldn't continue to have skin tests because the tests almost always will be positive from then on. Once you have a positive skin test, it's necessary to rely on symptoms to determine if you have tuberculosis. A chest radiograph should be obtained if you have a cough lasting for 2 to 3 weeks, if you are bringing up mucus with blood in it or if you have fever or weight loss. Routine yearly chest radiographs usually are not necessary.

Some people think that once they've been infected with the bacteria that causes tuberculosis, they don't need to take precautions or wear a mask when dealing with tuberculosis patients. Since there have been rare instances of persons being re-infected with a new tuberculosis strain, however, you should continue to take precautions.

Vendor Sign-in Procedures

All vendors must sign in any time they enter a hospital for any business-related purpose. Sign-in for representatives generally is completed at the Materials Management or Security departments immediately upon arrival. There will be a log documenting visits by vendors, and this vendor book must be signed with company name, contact information, and location to be visited/purpose of visit given. A visitor badge will be given at this time, and it is required that this badge and your company I.D. or name tag are visible at all times while in the hospital; a corporate photo I.D. is preferred.

On your first visit, you will most likely receive an information packet explaining the hospital's policies and procedures regarding vendors. If a packet is not provided, it is your responsibility to ask for information regarding policies and procedures for representatives.

It may be necessary to complete a supplier profile for the account prior to conducting any business meeting or transaction with the account, so you will want to be early for your first appointment at any new account.

Vendors must then check in with the respective department where an additional badge may be provided; this badge must also be visible at all times within the hospital.

If you will be entering an operating room or other invasive procedure room, representatives may be required to provide corporate documentation supporting their competency to use, demonstrate, and teach about their product.

Representatives are asked to leave the facility promptly upon completion of business.

Hospitals generally have different protocols that need to be adhered to after-hours. These will vary from hospital to hospital.

Prohibited Selling Activities

The hospital may have a policy stating that you may not show any other products or involve any other physicians or staff, except those with whom you have a set appointment.
Most hospitals request that sales calls to physicians are to be arranged through physicians' offices and that they take place in a non-patient care area. Many hospitals have policies requiring that only products already on the formulary be promoted to the physicians. Where this policy exists, the representative will need to work with the Pharmacist and Pharmacy and Therapeutics Committee to have a medication added to the formulary, prior to contacting any physicians who do not sit on the P & T Committee.

Most hospitals prohibit any promotion of products for an off-label use. You may promote your products only to physicians that are likely to prescribe them for approved indications. If you have a product cleared for use in treating allergic reactions, then you should restrict your sales to allergists and other physicians (such as family practice physicians) who are likely to prescribe medications to treat allergies. If you have a device cleared for use in spinal fusions only that has been used successfully by orthopedists in hip surgery you may only promote it to the spinal surgeons.

Competitive intelligence activities are strictly prohibited in most facilities. Representatives found inspecting or handling instruments owned by competitors or competitive product or literature risk being denied access to the O.R. and sterile processing areas, if not the entire account. Representatives should offer to leave the surgical suite when a competitive product is in use, even if both companies' products will be used during that same procedure. In some circumstances the surgical team may request that competing representatives are present at the same time.

The authorized agent of the HMO, GPO, or Central Purchasing Department must approve all contract negotiations. Finalized contracts may not be signed by anyone other than the appropriate administrative representative as defined by the healthcare provider. Representatives need to request information from their accounts regarding the contracting process. For hospital pharmaceutical sales, the best place to start this process is with the pharmacist, or Director of Pharmacy.

Failure to comply with any item within the institution's policies and procedures for vendors will result in the initiation of a supplier representative non-compliance protocol process. A non-compliant representative may be denied access to certain departments or to the facility as a whole either temporarily or indefinitely. Non-compliance by any company representative may jeopardize that company's status as a supplier to that institution. Certain non-compliance issues may result in criminal penalties or civil liabilities imposed upon the representative and/or the company.

<u>Supply and Delivery of Equipment & Instruments</u>

Deliveries by courier are to be directed to the entity receiving dock, and must be accompanied by a packing slip or receiving bill of lading with reference to a valid purchase order (P.O.). Receiving may refuse items delivered by courier without a valid

P.O. listed on the shipping label. Any instruments or equipment on loan must specify "LOANER" on the bill of lading – loaner instruments delivered by the representative may be exempt from a P.O. All equipment (including equipment on loan or consignment) must have a valid P.O. prior to being inspected by Biomedical.

Biomedical is open at most facilities from 7:00 am to 3:30 pm. Biomedical must be called to inspect any equipment prior to its use in the operating room. All equipment for biomedical inspection should be accompanied by owner's manual and any special instructions. Additionally, ALL accessories that can and/or will be utilized, such as adapters, power cords, etc should accompany equipment for biomedical inspection. Equipment must be UL approved. Each time a piece of equipment leaves the facility; it must be re-checked and approved by Biomedical when it is returned.

All equipment/instruments must be properly cleaned and decontaminated prior to delivery. Dirty instruments (with blood, bone, etc.) are not to be delivered. Detailed content checklists, set photos (Polaroid or digital camera print-outs are acceptable), and sterilization and decontamination instructions must be included for all consigned and loaned sets. Most institutions prefer that all instruments and equipment on loan, consignment, or evaluation be received and unpacked by the representative, and will be confirmed to have no missing or damaged items prior to delivery to the advanced clinician or charge nurse.

The representative will ensure delivery of loaned equipment or instruments to the advanced clinician or charge nurse (via Biomedical when appropriate) no less than 24 hours prior to the booked procedure start-time. The staff accepting the delivery will sign the count sheets. Some hospitals or surgery centers may prefer that instruments be checked in directly at the sterilization department (often referred to as the SPD or CPD).

Checking in Equipment and Instruments for Processing

- Provide appropriate sterilization containers - the weight of such containers shall not exceed 25 lbs.
- Assist the staff member in counting the implants and instruments on the count sheets, and request that the staff sign the count sheets.
- Provide photographs and sterilization instructions at this time, and communicate any special instructions.

Loaned instrument trays should be labeled with the company's name, tray name, physician name, and date of procedure and must be labeled "loaner" or "consignment."

At times a representative will be contacted to provide instruments or implants for an emergency procedure with little or no notice. In these situations, the equipment will often need to be delivered directly to the O.R. (at some facilities, to the central processing or SPD), and should be checked and signed for by a staff member of the facility if at all possible. There may be times where these steps are skipped due to the urgency of treating the patient.

Items lost or missing that were not signed for are the responsibility of the manufacturer – not the hospital.

Shipping containers are to be removed from hospital upon delivery of equipment and brought back at the time of removal. If storage space is required for shipping containers, approval from the charge nurse must be obtained, and should not exceed 24 hours under any circumstances. Flashing (sterilization) of additional implants and instruments may be against most hospitals' policies, and will usually be permitted only in emergencies. This is a patient safety issue!

Immediately following the procedure, walk the decontamination staff through the proper decontamination and disassembly procedures. Note any missing or damaged items, and attempt to locate missing items. Within 24 hours of decontamination, ensure that all sets are re-assembled and removed from the facility. Visually inspect all instruments and implants, and request additional cleaning as appropriate. At the time of removal the advanced clinician, sterile processing manager and the appropriate staff member responsible for creating the purchase order for the procedure must be notified of any missing or damaged items, and any potential charges

Flashing of instruments and implants is to be avoided whenever possible. Instruments provided sterile from other facilities within the same HMO or management group, which were transported with acceptable dust cover, may be utilized without additional processing at the discretion of the circulating nurse. Instruments provided sterile from any non-related facility must be re-processed prior to use, as different organizations have different policies and sterilization procedures. Sterilization, decontamination, and re-processing instructions must accompany equipment and instrument sets for emergency cases.

All products for review/evaluation generally need to be submitted through the O.R. Materials Management Department and/or the O.R. Purchasing Department. Some hospitals will request that the process be initiated directly with the hospital's centralized purchasing or materials management departments. O.R. purchasing and/or materials management will need to approve any introduction of a new product, and the advanced clinician or charge nurse must be notified. Any consumables used on a trial basis are to be without charge. Promotion of new products off-label to any physician or staff member is strictly prohibited by all facilities and by federal law.

No in-service or product demonstration will occur without prior knowledge and authorization. Authorization is usually obtained from the O.R. Education Coordinator, the O.R. Materials Management or Purchasing Manager, or the advanced clinician or charge nurse. Under no circumstances are products to be used on patients without the proper in-servicing to medical staff and healthcare providers. Failure to comply with product review/evaluation policies may jeopardize the supplier representative's ability to conduct future business with the account.

All contract negotiations must be approved by the facility's Central Materials Management Department or Purchasing Department. Finalized contracts may not be signed by anyone other than the appropriate administrative representative as defined by the healthcare provider. It is the responsibility of the representative to determine who the appropriate personnel are in each individual facility.

Review Question: No medical test is required prior to entering the hospital or institution. True or false?
Answer: False. A recent negative TB Test result must be provided to the institution's Materials Management prior to entering the facility (there may be different policies among hospitals on these issues). All representatives prior to entering the operating room, for their own safety, require Hepatitis B vaccination.

8. O.R. Protocol

Medical device representatives are likely to spend much of their time in one of the operating rooms or other procedure rooms.

When a surgeon requests the presence of a representative, it is the responsibility of the representative to request that the surgeon's office obtain written patient consent for the representative to attend the procedure. The O.R. Materials office and the appropriate charge nurse must be informed of any and all company reps (representatives) attending a procedure a minimum of 24 hours prior to the procedure (except for emergency cases). Any and all company representatives to attend must have completed all mandatory training and related requirements or permission to enter may be denied. Representatives are to coordinate the appropriate time of arrival with the charge nurse or circulating nurse prior to the start of the procedure.

Operating Room Attire

- Only greens provided by the hospital are to be worn when observing a procedure.
- Jewelry and additional clothing must be completely covered by greens or removed
- Nail polish and false nails are not permissible
- Head covering (bouffant style only – not skull cap), shoe-covers, mask, and eye-shield must be worn in the surgical suite
- High heels and open-toed shoes are not permitted
- Between cases, reps should change head cover, boot covers, mask, and eye shield
- For exceptionally close proximity to the patient, a face shield is recommended.

Review Question: Which of the following is correct when a surgeon requests the presence of a representative in the operating room?
a) It is the responsibility of the surgeon to request that the rep's office obtain written patient consent for the representative to attend the procedure.
b) It is the responsibility of the representative to request that the surgeon's office obtain written patient consent for the representative to attend the procedure.
c) It is the responsibility of the representative to request that the surgeon's office obtain written patient consent for the representative to attend the procedure.
Answer: b

Ask permission prior to utilizing any O.R. phone, and keep calls brief regarding necessary business only. Cellular phones may be utilized in the O.R. area for emergencies only. Do NOT use cell phones in the surgical suite. Cell phones with cameras may not be utilized anywhere in the O.R. area or locker rooms. Never give out O.R. phone numbers for the purpose of receiving personal calls while in the O.R. Cell phones and pagers must be in vibrate mode or turned off when in the surgical suite.

Most hospitals will not allow representatives to scrub for cases under any circumstances, and they must remain at least 1 foot (preferably 3 feet) away from the sterile field at all times. They should avoid touching skin, face, and nose. They should wash hands for a minimum of 20 seconds with antimicrobial soap (antimicrobial soaps contain substances that reduce the number of bacterial flora) as follows:

- After handling shipping containers and/or unsterile instruments or equipment
- Prior to donning greens

- Before entering and upon leaving the surgical suite
- Before and after utilizing the restroom
- Before and after eating
- After removing gloves or mask
- After touching nose, mouth, or eyes

Improved adherence to hand hygiene (i.e., hand washing or use of alcohol-based hand rubs) has been shown to terminate outbreaks in health care facilities, to reduce transmission of antimicrobial resistant organisms (e.g. methicillin-resistant staphylococcus aureus), and reduce overall infection rates. In addition to traditional hand washing with soap and water, Centers for Disease Control (CDC) recommends the use of alcohol-based hand rubs by health care personnel for patient care.

The use of gloves does not eliminate the need for hand hygiene. Likewise, the use of hand hygiene does not eliminate the need for gloves. Gloves reduce hand contamination by 70 percent to 80 percent, prevent cross-contamination and protect patients and health care personnel from infection. Healthcare workers should use hand rubs before and after each patient, just as gloves should be changed before and after each patient.

When using an alcohol-based hand rub, apply the product to the palm of one hand and rub the hands together, while covering all surfaces of hands and fingers, until the hands are dry. Note that the volume needed to reduce the number of bacteria on hands varies by product. Alcohol-based hand rubs significantly reduce the number of microorganisms on skin, are fast-acting, and cause less skin irritation.

Health care personnel should avoid wearing artificial nails and keep natural nails less than one quarter of an inch long if they care for patients at high risk of acquiring infections. Many hospitals no longer permit any member of the surgical team to wear false nails, nail polish, or to keep long natural nails.

O.R. Etiquette

The rep should arrive at the facility with plenty of time available to sign-in with Materials Management, Security, and the O.R. Report to the circulating nurse upon arrival and provide correct spelling of his or her name and company name for medical records. The rep should enter the O.R. only when his product is in use, and leave upon completion of that use. Only one representative may be in the O.R. at any given time except with prior approval. Training of new company representatives is to take place at company sponsored training, NOT in the O.R.

Briefcases, purses, and computer bags are not permitted in the operating or procedure room. Reps are not to enter the doctor's lounge. Although a physician may invite the rep in from time to time, other physicians utilizing the room may not want representatives in the doctors' lounge, and therefore the rep should not enter even if invited. The rep should minimize phone calls and visits to the O.R. desk and enter a sterile instrument storage area at the request of a circulating nurse or charge nurse only. The rep should minimize time spent in the nurses' lounge, and vacate during lunch hour and other busy times. Reps are not permitted behind the O.R. desk. Reps are NOT to enter the recovery room.

The rep should keep conversation directly related to the use of his product for the specific procedure and patient during the procedure. He should advise the surgical team in the safe and effective use of equipment and instruments only as needed. Verbal instructions for assembly of instruments are fine. The rep may provide appropriate sterile packaged devices to the circulating nurse to open as needed, answer technical questions, assist in trouble shooting if problems arise, assess product performance, utilize surgical team assessment to make improvements, and advise on disassembly of instruments as needed.

Problem	Solution
Conversation increases risk of transmission of pathogens.	Minimize conversation.
The patient even when anesthetized may hear conversations.	Keep conversations professional.
Double masking prevents airflow through the mask and thus increases potential spread of infection.	Wear only one mask.
Any movement in the room increases the potential for nosocomial (hospital-induced) infection	Minimize movement.
Opening of the O.R. doors releases the positive pressure in the O.R. leading to increased potential for nosocomial infection	Opening of doors should be kept to a minimum.

Movement is to be front-to-front or back-to-back. Never turn your back to the sterile field or to a sterile surgical team member. Unsterile personnel do not move between sterile fields. Unsterile personnel should never move between laminar flow and the sterile field.

Unsterile personnel should remain a minimum of 3 feet away from any sterile surface or object, and should never reach over any sterile surface or object. Have a laser pointer available for pointing at sterile instruments and implants. Do NOT touch any sterile attire, drapes, surfaces, or objects. Do NOT open sterile packaging under any circumstances. Do NOT assist in the gowning of sterile personnel.

Do NOT operate or adjust any equipment (except to perform specifically exempted procedures such as remote calibration of lasers, pacemakers, etc). Ensure that staff are trained prior to procedures in the operation of any equipment; during procedures offer verbal instruction on the operation of any equipment or instruments. Exceptions to the operation of unsterile equipment may be made with respect to:

- Specially trained company technicians contracted to provide service to the facility
- Suppliers whose credentials have been assessed and verified by the O.R. Materials Manager, advanced clinician, or nurse educator AND then only when under direct supervision of a staff RN

Do NOT sell or market during the observation of a procedure:

- This activity is distracting to the physician and staff
- Marketing and selling for future cases demonstrates a lack of consideration for the current patient
- Additional conversation, movement, and demonstrations increase the risk of contamination of the sterile field, and increase potential for nosocomial infection
- It is simply unprofessional behavior and will lead to loss of respect for the representative by the surgical team

While in the department you may show only the product approved for use that day by a particular surgeon and on a particular patient. Do not show any other products or involve any other physicians or patients. Sales calls to physicians are to be arranged through physicians' offices and should take place in a non-patient care area.

Failure to comply with any item within a facilities guidelines and policies pertaining to suppliers may result in the initiation of the supplier representative non-compliance protocol process. A non-compliant representative may be denied access to certain departments or to the facility as a whole either temporarily or indefinitely. Non-compliance by any company representative may jeopardize that company's status as a supplier to the facility or to the HMO. Certain non-compliance issues may result in criminal penalties or civil liabilities imposed upon the supplier.

Review Question: Training of new company representatives is to take place:
a) At company sponsored training
b) In the O.R.
c) Wherever the rep wants to be trained
Answer: a

9. Infectious Disease & Bloodborne Pathogens

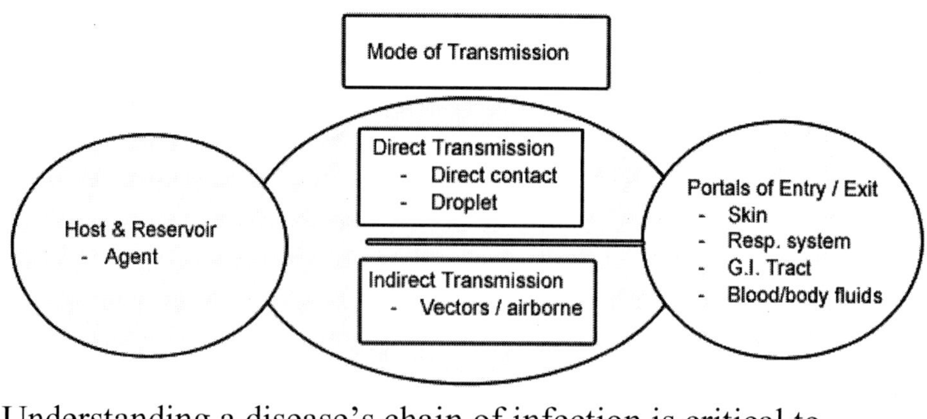

Understanding a disease's chain of infection is critical to control or prevent the spread of disease successfully. An infectious disease cannot spread when one of the connections in the chain is broken. Hand washing, protective equipment and clothing, sterilization, special waste disposal mechanisms, isolation, and vaccinations are some examples of ways the chain of infection is broken in the healthcare setting.

Bloodborne pathogens of greatest concern to medical sales representatives include HIV (Human Immunodeficiency Virus), HBV (Hepatitis B Virus), and HCV (Hepatitis C Virus). Bloodborne pathogens are generally transmitted by direct contact with blood from an infected person to the mucous membranes or broken skin of the previously uninfected person. Airborne pathogens include tuberculosis, chickenpox, and measles. These airborne transmitted diseases are most commonly spread by coughing, talking, or breathing, since the disease is spread by bacteria that are released into the air. Additionally, staph (staphylococcus) bacteria and MRSA (methicillin-resistant Staphylococcus aureus) are spread from person to person by droplets of infected secretions from the mouth and nose, through sneezing or coughing. (They may also be spread by skin contact.) Staph infections acquired during surgery can be very serious. Staph bacteria and MRSA can be found on the skin and in the nose of some people without causing illness.

A nosocomial infection is one that arises after 48 hours of hospitalization.

"Universal precautions," as defined by CDC, are a set of precautions designed to prevent transmission of bloodborne pathogens when providing first aid or health care. Under universal precautions, blood and certain body fluids of all patients are considered potentially infectious for bloodborne pathogens. Implementing universal precautions does not eliminate the need for other isolation precautions, such as droplet precautions for influenza, airborne isolation for pulmonary tuberculosis, or contact isolation for methicillin-resistant Staphylococcus aureus.

The CDC guidelines include six standard precautions for preventing the spread of infection in the O.R. setting:

1. Hand washing
2. Protective equipment and attire (gloves, masks, eyewear, gowns)
3. Special handling of patient care equipment and linens
4. Cleaning and disinfecting environmental surfaces
5. Preventing sharps-related injuries
6. Using ventilating devices

Patients in the operating room have a compromised immunity due to the incision alone, in addition to any additional health problems they may have. Therefore, it is important that the sales representative take precautions in consideration of the patient. This means not being in the O.R. if ill.

As a health care worker, you may be exposed to many different sources of infection. Infections may be transmitted by blood or body fluids, by air or respiratory secretions, or by direct contact with other infectious materials. You can protect yourself from infection by using personal protective equipment like gloves and masks, and by following universal precautions (that is, handling all blood and body fluids as if they are infectious). Dispose of used needles and other sharp disposable instruments in appropriate sharps disposal containers. Hepatitis B vaccination is also recommended for all healthcare workers and medical sales representatives. Additionally, frequent hand washing with antimicrobial soap is crucial.

Body fluids such as tears, sweat, saliva, urine, and vomitus are not thought to transmit bloodborne pathogens unless they are visibly contaminated with blood. (Urine or fecal material may contain bacteria or infectious agents that are not considered bloodborne pathogens.) Most other body fluids, such as semen, vaginal secretions and pericardial, peritoneal, joint, amniotic, and cerebrospinal fluids, can transmit bloodborne pathogens.

The guidelines below can help you protect yourself from bloodborne infections:

- Follow universal precautions - consider every patient to be infected.
- Avoid contact with the blood or body fluids of all patients.
- Avoid risky behavior when using needles and other sharp instruments, including scissors, scalpels, blades, and knives. For example, don't recap needles. Carefully dispose of sharp instruments in appropriate containers.
- Wear protective equipment, including gloves and face shields, to avoid getting blood on your skin or in your eyes when you're observing procedures that may cause splashes or spills, or when you are assisting with the decontamination of your instruments.
- Be certain you are immunized against hepatitis B

Immediately following an exposure to blood:

- Wash needle sticks and cuts with soap and water
- Flush splashes to the nose, mouth, or skin with water
- Irrigate eyes with clean water, saline, or sterile irrigants

No scientific evidence shows that using antiseptics or squeezing the wound will reduce the risk of transmission of a blood borne pathogen. Using a caustic agent such as bleach is not recommended.

Following any blood exposure you should report the exposure to the circulating nurse, who should then ensure that the appropriate departments will be notified, and that the hospital's post-exposure plan can is activated. If your skin is broken (by a needle-stick) or fluid has splashed into your eyes, your mouth, or onto broken skin, both you and the source patient will be tested. Blood tests should verify that you're immune to hepatitis B and don't currently have a blood-borne infection. The source patient's current and past infections will also be checked.

If the source patient is infected with hepatitis B and, despite immunization, you never developed immunity to hepatitis B, you will be given hepatitis B immune globulin. If the source patient has syphilis, you will be offered antibiotics. If the source patient has HIV infection, you may take preventive medicines for four weeks. These medicines should be started within hours of the accident. You will have repeat blood tests for 6 to 9 months, depending on the risks posed by the source patient. Thus, if any infection develops, it will be found as soon as possible.

If your skin has no breaks, cracks or rashes, you have virtually no risk of getting a bloodborne infection despite the splash of blood. If you do receive an exposure to your skin, immediately wash the affected area thoroughly. For a very small splash, you may request an alcohol prep pad from the anesthesiologist or circulating nurse.

The surgical mask protects the mucous membranes of the nose and mouth from contact with microorganisms. A surgical mask protects against exposure to large-particle droplet spatter (larger than 5 microns in size) that may contain bloodborne pathogens or other infectious microorganisms. When a surgical mask is used, it should be changed between patients or during patient treatment if it becomes wet. The 1991 Occupational Safety and

Health Administration Bloodborne Pathogens Final Rule mandates wearing masks in specified circumstances to reduce the risk of exposures to blood borne pathogens.

Healthcare personnel should wear protective eyewear with solid side shields during procedures and patient-care activities likely to generate splashes or sprays of blood or body fluids. Protective eyewear provides protection of the mucous membranes of the eyes from contact with microorganisms. Reusable facial personal protective equipment should be disinfected between patients. The 1991 Occupational Safety and Health Administration Blood borne Pathogens Final Rule mandates wearing eye protection in specified circumstances to reduce the risk of exposures to blood borne pathogens.

Protective eyewear with solid side shields and a surgical mask are adequate for procedures where small amounts of spatter or splashes are likely. Adding a face shield may be useful when more protection is desired during procedures where blood splatter is likely due to the use of surgical drills, hammering of press-fit implants or distractors/dilators, and so on.

Various types of protective apparel (e.g., gowns, jackets) are worn to provide barrier protection and to reduce opportunities for transmission of microorganisms in healthcare settings. Gowns are worn to prevent contamination of clothing and to protect the skin of personnel from exposure to blood and body fluids. When the gown is worn as personal protective equipment (i.e., when spatter and spray of blood, saliva, or other potentially infectious material is anticipated), the sleeve length should be long. Protective apparel should be changed daily, or sooner if visibly soiled. The 1991 Occupational Safety and Health Administration Bloodborne Pathogens Final Rule mandates wearing protective apparel in specified circumstances to reduce the risk of exposures to bloodborne pathogens.

Healthcare personnel wear gloves to provide a protective barrier and to prevent contamination of the hands when touching mucous membranes, blood, saliva, or other potentially infectious materials. Medical sales representatives should wear gloves when they are observing a procedure, as it is possible for surfaces of tables and equipment to become contaminated with blood or other bodily fluids. Additionally, when handling implants and instruments prior to sterilization (including after decontamination or washing) gloves should be worn. The washer does not necessarily clean all cannulas or threads of screws or other less obvious areas. Only after sterilization is it safe to handle these devices without gloves. Many healthcare facilities will run loaned instruments through a washer, but will not actually sterilize the trays. It is recommended that you request that the trays be sterilized prior to being removed from the facility, for the protections of all persons who may come into contact with the trays.

The U.S. Department of Labor Occupational Safety and Health Administration is responsible for Regulations regarding Occupational Exposure to Bloodborne Pathogens and other infectious disease risk to healthcare workers. For more information on these topics, or for a copy of the regulations regarding Occupational Exposure to Bloodborne Pathogens (29 CFR Part 1910) visit www.osha.gov.

Review Question: If blood splashes on your skin in the O.R., you will DEFINITELY ALWAYS get sick from a bloodborne infection. True or false?
Answer: False

Review Question: The FDA is responsible for regulations regarding occupational exposure to bloodborne pathogens and other infectious disease risk to healthcare workers. True or false?
Answer: False

10. Occupational Safety

Back injuries are the most common injuries that occur in the workplace. Back injuries may be acute or chronic in nature, and an acute injury always has the potential to become chronic. Back injuries are also cumulative in nature, and may develop slowly over time. Lifting, pushing, pulling, repetitive tasks, and static or awkward postures may cause back injuries.

Medical sales representatives are frequently required to lift and move heavy equipment and instrument trays. They are also often required to do so while wearing expensive clothing. This is a dangerous combination. Representatives should consider saving the expensive suits for days when they have important meetings, and wear more durable professional attire day to day.

Lifting hints:

- When lifting, it is important to determine the approximate weight of the object, where it is located, what shape the object is, what the contents is are inside, and if shifting of the contents is likely to occur inside the package.
- Determine how you will lift the package and where you want to place it.
- Maintain natural spinal curves.
- Use a wide base of support with feet diagonally placed, shoulder width apart. Flex at hips and knees only--do not flex the trunk forward.

- Bring the object as close as possible to your center of gravity (navel) as possible.
- When turning, use your feet and do NOT twist your trunk.
- Ask for help if needed.
- Ensure you have proper equipment available for lifting large and heavy objects.
- Consider use of a back support when you will be delivering or picking up heavy trays or equipment.

Pushing and Pulling Tasks

- Push – don't pull, if possible
- Use your legs and not your back (especially when pushing)
- Move close to the object
- Keep elbows bent and close to your sides
- Maintain natural spinal curvatures
- Use a smooth and controlled motion rather than a quick jerking action to initiate movement

Reaching Tasks

- Establish a stable base of support with feet diagonal and knees bent
- Avoid stretching or twisting for an object – use a taller step, get assistance, move objects that may be blocking it
- When lifting overhead, make the load lighter, keep feet apart, and use a ladder or platform
- Get assistance for heavier objects
- Use a ladder or platform if you must lift an object to a height above your shoulders
- Bend your knees if reaching below your knees
- If you must reach across a table, use one arm to brace yourself, if possible

Continuously standing in one position during lengthy surgical procedures causes muscle fatigue and pooling of blood in the lower extremities. Standing on hard surfaces such as concrete creates trauma and pain to the feet. Awkward postures such as tilting your head down for a long period of time can cause muscle fatigue as well. The best solutions are as follows:

- Change position frequently if possible
- Use a stool to sit where possible, and use a footrest or bar to raise or reposition feet periodically
- Wear shoes with well cushioned insteps and soles

Review Question: Which of the following is NOT a way to avoid stretching or twisting for an object?
a) Lean as far as you can toward the object
b) Use a taller step.
c) Get assistance.
d) Move objects that may be blocking the object.
Answer: a

Biohazardous Waste Disposal

Biohazardous waste includes:

- Sharps (any device capable of cutting or piercing the skin)
- Microbiological such as cultures and stocks
- Pathological such as human tissue or organs
- Body substances
- Blood and blood products including any material that contains fluid blood or blood products, releases liquid blood when compressed, or is dried and heavily caked

Biohazardous waste must be handled in a separate waste stream from the point of origin to disposal. Proper disposal to the appropriate toilet, hopper or container is very important.

Biohazardous waste must be transported in a covered rigid leak resistant container, and must NEVER be transported in a regular trashcan or linen cart, nor should it be stored on the floor in a red bag (hospitals will have red biohazardous waste bags for disposal of certain types of biohazardous materials). Once the waste is placed in the red bag or the sharps container, NEVER put your hands in the red bag or sharps container.

California State Law requires that pharmaceutical waste must be segregated and handled in a separate waste stream from point of origin to disposal. Pharmaceutical waste is defined as non-intact, damaged, contaminated or otherwise unwanted medications. Pharmaceutical waste may be hazardous or non-hazardous. Pharmaceutical waste containers are unique and must be used according to specific guidelines. There are four types of Pharmaceutical waste containers:

- Medications
- IV Bags/Bottles
- Resource Conservation and Recovery Act (RCRA) containers
- Chemotherapeutic waste

Pharmaceutical waste containers will be placed in a hazardous materials storage area for removal and incineration by the appropriate licensed waste hauler.

In the operating room, it is the responsibility of the hospital staff to dispose of any such waste. Do not attempt to be helpful by throwing away any waste unless you have been asked to AND you know what the proper disposal method is for the particular item.

Chemical Spills

Do NOT handle hazardous substances without training. Proper training will include proper storage and handling and good transportation practices; use and location of spill kits, use and location of Personal Protective Equipment (PPE).

Should a Spill Occur: Certain spills require an emergency spill response because they pose a significant threat to health and safety. The circulating nurse should be informed that he/she may activate the hospital's emergency procedures for chemical spills if necessary. If possible, inform her of the chemical's identity. Generally speaking, if you did not provide the product that was spilled, the best reaction by a sales representative is to inform the circulating nurse or appropriate staff member, and stay clear of the spill. If you provided the product, you should have Material Safety Data Sheets (MSDS) available, and be able to offer advice and information regarding the substance and best methods for cleaning up the spill.

Review Question: Which of the following is the correct way for a device representative to react to an unidentified chemical spill?
a) Immediately get some paper towels and wipe it up.
b) Ignore it and just go about your sales business.
c) Inform the circulating nurse or appropriate staff member, and stay clear of the spill.
Answer: c

Electrical Safety

All pieces of electronically operated equipment introduced to the hospital must be inspected and cleared by Engineering and/or Biomedical. This applies to any equipment leased, borrowed, rented, demonstrated, or otherwise introduced on a permanent or temporary basis. All electrical equipment shall carry the UL label or have other appropriate safety certification. Any electrical equipment used in the area of direct care of the patient must be equipped with a three-prong electrical plug that is of a hospital grade. (The plug will have a green dot.) Equipment that is double insulated does not require a cord and plug as described above.

Extension Cords, Power Strips, and Adapters:

- Single outlet extension cords may only be used with the permission of the safety officer or operations supervisor. They shall be removed from service as soon as possible.
- Hospital grade power strips may be used.
- The use of multi-outlet adapters is prohibited.

Radiation Safety

Exposure of medical representatives to radiation can occur from portable and fixed X-ray machines and fluoroscopy machines used in the operating room, interventional radiology, or interventional cardiology suites. Potential health effects of radiation exposure are somatic (body) or genetic (offspring) in nature. Radiation exposure occurs when unprotected personnel are near a machine in operation. The degree of exposure depends on the amount of radiation, the duration of exposure, the distance from the source, and the type of shielding in place.

Acute exposure is very rare due to the advancements of radiology equipment in modern facilities. An acute exposure may result in erythema and dermatitis. Large whole-body exposures cause nausea, vomiting, diarrhea, weakness, and death.

Chronic exposure is, however, a possibility for some medical representatives, as they are frequently exposed to radiation on a daily basis for certain products. Chronic exposure may lead to skin cancer and bone marrow suppression. Genetic effects may lead to congenital defects in the exposed person's offspring.

Persons frequently exposed to radiation may wear film badges for personal exposure monitoring. Medical device representatives do generally not utilize these badges, but this is not necessarily correct. Orthopedic Surgeons are generally required to wear such badges, and certain representatives may in fact be receiving more exposure than some orthopedic surgeons.

Radiation safety precautions are:

- Time – limit and decrease length of time spent near the radiation source.
- Distance – Step at least 6 feet away from the source of radiation
- Shielding – Shield yourself from radiation

In order to prevent chronic exposures, the best practices for medical device representatives who are exposed regularly to radiation are as follows:

- Leave the room during imaging whenever possible
- If you must be in the room, always wear a lead apron and thyroid protection
- If you are in the room, in addition to wearing lead or standing behind a lead shield, you can attempt to stand at least 6 feet away from the source (the farther the better).
- Medical representatives who are pregnant should take special care in following these precautions.

<u>Work Related Injuries or Incidents</u>

Work related injuries or incidents must be reported immediately to the department manager or supervisor in charge within 24 hours. All employees, volunteers, and students have the immediate responsibility for their own safety, and that of other personnel who may be affected by their actions. This responsibility includes the use of personal protective equipment issued in the prescribed manner to provide protection from potential hazards. As a sales representative working in the hospital, you are required to report any injury or incident as though you are an employee of the facility.

If you are injured yourself, you will also need to inform your own direct supervisor within 24 hours. If necessary, report to the Emergency Department for treatment. You will be required to provide all appropriate information to your employer, including and work limitations resulting from your injury. Your employer may require you to present a doctor's release upon return to work. Your employer may also direct you to certain physicians for assessment for your employer's Worker's Compensation insurance provider.

Review Question: As a sales representative working in the hospital, you are required to report any injury or incident as though you are an employee of the facility. True or false?
Answer: True

Emergency Preparedness

Facilities will often have an internal number to dial on hospital phone lines in order to report emergencies. If you are not aware of that code, default to 911 but note that you may need to access an outside line in order to make a successful 911 call.
If you detect a fire or smoke:
R -- remove any persons in immediate danger

A -- activate the alarm (pull station or use an outside line to dial 911)
C -- contain the fire
E -- evacuate behind smoke barriers

If you receive a call with a bomb threat:

- Get as much information as possible from the caller
- Keep the caller on the line as long as possible
- Listen for background noises
- Dial the designated emergency number as listed above to report the situation

Emergency codes will vary from one facility to another. The following are examples of emergency codes from a particular hospital:

Fire	**red**
Unruly patient or family member	**green**
Person with a weapon	**yellow**
Person having a heart attack	**blue**
Infant abduction	**purple**

11. AdvaMed Code of Ethics

Written by the Advanced Medical Technology Association in September 2003, the AdvaMed Code of Ethics is supported by several major medical device manufacturers including (but not limited to) Medtronic Sofamor Danek, Zimmer Holdings, Inc., Smith & Nephew, Inc., Stryker Corporation, Biomet, Inc. and Depuy Inc.

AdvaMed recognizes that its members may interact with health care professionals for many legitimate objectives other than selling, leasing, recommending, arranging for the sale or lease of, or prescribing products, and that some of these relationships are not addressed in the code of ethics. Any interpretation of the provisions of this Code as well as AdvaMed's members' interactions with health care professionals not specifically addressed in this Code, should be made in light of the following principle: AdvaMed members shall encourage ethical business practices and socially responsible industry conduct and shall not use any unlawful inducement in order to sell, lease, recommend, or arrange for the sale, lease, or prescription of their products.

AdvaMed adopted this voluntary Code of Ethics effective January 1, 2004 to facilitate Members' ethical interactions with Health Care Professionals in the United States.

(For the purposes of this section, the term "members" will refer to the medical device manufacturers and biotechnology and pharmaceutical companies belonging to AdvaMed.)

Developing cutting edge medical technology and improving existing products are collaborative processes between members and health care professionals. Innovation and creativity are essential to the development and evolution of medical devices, and often occur outside the laboratories of medical device companies. Heart valves, MRI equipment, cardiac rhythm devices, surgical tools, and infusion pumps are just a few examples of the array of complex medical technologies developed through research collaborations and consulting relationships between health care professionals and medical manufacturers.

The safe and effective use of sophisticated electronic, in vitro diagnostic, surgical, or other medical technology often requires medical manufacturers to offer health care professionals appropriate instruction, education, training, service and technical support. Regulators may also require this type of training as a condition of product approval.

Medical device manufacturers' support of bona fide medical research, education and enhancement of professional skills serves patient safety and increases access t new technology.

AdvaMed members have a responsibility to make product education and training available to health care professionals. The U.S. Food and Drug Administration mandates training and education to facilitate the safe and effective use of certain medical technology. Such programs often occur at centralized locations (necessitating out-of-town travel for some participants), and may last more than one day. Member programs focused on the education and training in the safe and effective use of medical products should be conducted as follows:

- Programs and events should be conducted in clinical, educational, conference, or other settings, including hotel of other commercially available meeting facilities, conducive to the effective transmission of knowledge.
- Programs requiring "hands on" training in medical procedures should be held at training facilities, medical institutions, laboratories, or other appropriate facilities. The training staff should have the proper qualifications and expertise to conduct such training.
- Members may provide health care professional attendees with hospitality only in the form of modest meals and receptions in connection with these programs. Any such meals and receptions should be modest in value and subordinate in time and focus to the educational or training purpose of the meeting.

- Members may pay for reasonable travel and modest lodging costs incurred by attending health care professionals.
- It is not appropriate for members to pay for the meals, hospitality, travel, or other expenses for guests of health care professionals or for any other person who does not have a bona fide professional interest in the information being shared at the meeting.

Bona fide independent, educational, scientific, or policy-making conferences promote scientific knowledge, medical advancement, and the delivery of effective health care. These typically include conferences sponsored by national, regional, or specialty medical associations, conferences sponsored by accredited continuing medical education providers, and grand rounds. Members may support these conferences in various ways.

Members may provide a grant either directly to the conference sponsor to reduce conference costs, or to a training institution or the conference sponsor to allow attendance by medical students, residents, fellows, and others who are health care professionals in training. Members may provide educational grants when:

- The gathering is primarily dedicated to promoting objective scientific and educational activities and discourse; and
- The training institution or the conference sponsor selects the attending health care professionals who are in training.

Such grants should be paid only to organizations with a genuine educational purpose or function, and may be used only to reimburse the legitimate expenses for bona fide educational activities. Such grants also should be consistent with relevant guidelines established by professional societies or organizations. The conference sponsor should be responsible for and control the selection of program content, faculty, educational methods, and materials.

Members may provide funding to the conference sponsor to support the conference's meals and hospitality. Also, members themselves may provide meals and receptions for all health care professional attendees, but only if it is provided in a manner that is also consistent with the sponsor's guidelines. Any meals, receptions, and hospitality should be modest in value and should be subordinate in time and focus to the purpose of the conference.

Members may make grants to conference sponsors for reasonable honoraria, travel, lodging, and meals for health care professionals who are bona fide conference faculty members.

Members may purchase advertisements and lease booth space for company displays at conferences.

It is appropriate for members to meet with health care professionals to discuss product features, contract negotiations, and sales terms. It is appropriate for members to pay for occasional hospitality only in the form of modest meals and receptions for health care professional attendees that are conducive to the exchange of information. It is also appropriate to pay for reasonable travel costs of attendees when necessary (i.e., for plant tours or demonstrations of non-portable equipment).

Many health care professionals serve as consultants to members, and provide valuable bona fide consulting services, including research, participation on advisory boards, presentations at member-sponsored training, and product collaboration. It is appropriate to pay Health Care Professionals reasonable compensation for performing these services. The following factors support the existence of a bona fide consulting arrangement between members and health care professionals:

- Member consulting arrangements should be written, signed by the parties, and specify all services to be provided.
- Compensation paid to consultants should be consistent with fair market value for the services provided.
- Consulting agreements should be entered into only where a legitimate need and purpose for the services is identified in advance.
- Selection of consultants should be on the basis of the consultant's qualifications and expertise to address the identified purpose, and should not be on the basis of volume or value of business generated by the consultant.
- The venue and circumstances for member meetings with consultants should be conducted in clinical, educational, conference, or other setting, including hotel or other commercially available meeting facilities, conducive to the effective exchange of information.
- Member-sponsored hospitality that occurs in conjunction with a consultant meeting should be modest in value and should be subordinate in time and focus to the primary purpose of the meeting.
- Members may pay reasonable and actual expenses incurred by consultants in carrying out the subject of the consulting arrangement, including reasonable and actual travel, modest meals and lodging costs incurred y consultants attending meetings with , or on behalf of, members.

- When a Member contracts with a consultant for research services, there should be a written research protocol.

Members occasionally may provide modest gifts to health care professionals, but only if the gifts benefit patients or serve a genuine educational function. Other than the gift of medical textbooks or anatomical models used for educational purposes, any gift from a member should have a fair market value of less than $100.

In addition, members may occasionally give health care professionals branded promotional items of minimal value related to the health care professional's work of for the benefit of patients. Gifts may not be given in the form of cash or cash equivalents.

This section is not intended to address the legitimate practice of providing appropriate sample products and opportunities for product evaluation.

Members may support accurate and responsible billing to Medicare and other payers by providing reimbursement information to health care providers regarding members' products, including identifying appropriate coverage, coding, or billing of member products, or of procedures using those products. Members may also provide information designed to offer technical or other support intended to aid in the appropriate and efficient use of installation of the member's products. However, it is inappropriate for members to provide this technical or other support for the purpose of unlawfully inducing health care professionals to purchase, lease, recommend, use, or arrange for the purchase, lease, or prescription of members' products.

Members may make donations for a charitable purpose, such as supporting genuine independent medical research for the advancement of medical science or education, indigent care, patient education, public education, or the sponsorship of events where proceeds are intended for charitable purposes. Donations should be made only to charitable organizations or, in rare instances, to individuals engaged in genuine charitable missions for the support of that mission. It is not appropriate for members to make such donations fort the purpose of unlawfully inducing health care professionals to purchase, lease, recommend, use, or arrange for the purchase, lease, or prescription of members' products. All donations should be appropriately documented. Examples of appropriate charitable grants and related considerations are:

--Advancement of Medical Education

Members may make grants to support the genuine medical education of medial students, residents, and fellows participating in fellowship programs, which are charitable or have an academic affiliation or other medical personnel.

--Support of Research with Scientific Merit

Members may make research grants to support genuine medical research. The purpose of the grant must be clearly documented.

--Public Education

Members may make grants for the purpose of supporting education of patients or the public about important health care topics and regulations. The information provided by the Department of Health and Human Services, Office of the Inspector General, as well as applicable laws or regulations, may provide more details than this Code, and members should address any additional questions to their own attorneys. This Code of Ethics is intended to facilitate ethical behavior, and is not intended t be, nor should it be, construed as legal advice. The Code is not intended to define or create legal rights, standards, or obligations.

Review Question: Which of the following is NOT a correct way for AvaMed members to financially support educational, scientific, or policy-making conferences?
a) To individuals and companies that are prospective customers or clients
b) To the conference sponsor to reduce conference costs
c) To a training institution
d) To the conference sponsor to allow attendance by medical students, residents, fellows, and others who are health care professionals in training
Answer: a

Review Question: Which of the following is true about the relationship between members and the health care professionals who serve as consultants to them?
a) It is appropriate to pay health care professionals reasonable compensation for performing these services.
b) It is NOT appropriate to pay health care professionals reasonable compensation for performing these services.
c) It doesn't matter one way or the other whether or not members pay health care professionals reasonable compensation for performing these services.
Answer: a

12. FDA Regulations for Medical Devices

FDA's Center for Devices and Radiological Health (CDRH) is responsible for regulating firms that manufacture, repackage, relabel, and/or import medical devices sold in the United States. In addition, CDRH regulates radiation-emitting electronic products (medical and non-medical) such as lasers, x-ray systems, ultrasound equipment, microwave ovens, and color televisions.

Medical devices are classified into Class I, II, and III. Regulatory control increases from Class I to Class III. The device classification regulation defines the regulatory requirements for a general device type. Most Class I devices are exempt from Premarket Notification 510(k); most Class II devices require Premarket Notification 510 (k); and most Class III devices require Premarket Approval. A description of device classifications and product classification databases can be found at http://www.fda.gov/cdrh/devadvice/313.html

The basic regulatory requirements that manufacturers of medical devices distributed in the U.S. must comply with are…

- Premarket Notification 510(k), unless exempt, or Premarket Approval (PMA)
- Establishment registration on form FDA_2891
- Medical Device Listing on form FDA_2892
- Quality System regulation
- Labeling Requirements
- Medical Device Reporting

Review Question: What is the name of the section of the FDA that is responsible for regulating firms that manufacture, repackage, relabel, and/or import medical devices sold in the United States?
a) Center for Biological and Sociological Health (CBSH)
b) Center for Devices and Radiological Health (CDRH)
c) Center for Astronomical and Spatial Health (CASH)
Answer: b

Definitions and Acronyms

Application Integrity Policy (AIP)
Application Integrity Policy (AIP) is FDA's policy for the integrity of data or information submitted in an application. If it

is suspected that an applicant has submitted false or misleading information, the data are thoroughly investigated. Submitting false or misleading information may result in FDA refusal to review submissions until certain requirements are met.

Implant
An implant is a device that is placed into a surgically or naturally formed cavity of the human body with the intention to remain there for 30 days or more. In order to protect public health, FDA may determine that devices placed in subjects for shorter periods are also implants.

Institutional Review Board (IRB)
Institutional Review Board (IRB) is a board, committee, or other group formally designated by an institution to review, to approve the initiation of, and to conduct periodic review of biomedical research involving human subjects. The primary purpose of such review is to assure the protection of the rights, safety, and welfare of human subjects. The IRB should be established, operated, and function in conformance with 21 CFR 56. The term has the same meaning as "institutional review committee" in section 520(g) of the FD&C Act.

Investigation
Investigation is a clinical investigation or research involving one or more subjects to determine the safety and/or effectiveness of a device.

Investigational device
Investigational device is a device, including a transitional device, which is the object of an investigation.

Investigational device exemptions (IDE)
IDE refers to the regulations of 21 CFR 812. An approved IDE means that the IRB (and FDA for significant risk devices) has approved the sponsor's study application and all the requirements under 21 CFR 812 are met.

Investigator
Investigator is an individual who actually conducts a clinical investigation, i.e., under whose immediate direction the investigational device is administered, dispensed, or used. In the event of an investigation being conducted by a team of individuals, "investigator" refers to the responsible leader of that team.

Monitor
When used as a noun, "monitor" is an individual designated by a sponsor or contract research organization to oversee the progress of an investigation. The monitor may be an employee of a sponsor, or a consultant to the sponsor, or an employee of or consultant to a contract research organization. When used as a verb, "monitor" means to oversee an investigation.

Premarket Approval (PMA)
A Premarket approval means any premarket approval application for a Class III medical device, including all information submitted with or incorporated by reference therein. (21 CFR 814.3)

Premarket Notification [PMN or 510(k)]
510(k) refers to the type of submission to FDA described under 21 CFR 807 Subpart E in which the applicant must establish that its device is substantially equivalent to a legally marketed device. This type of submission is used for most Class II devices and some Class I devices.

Significant risk device (SR device)
Significant risk device is an investigational device that: (1) is intended as an implant and presents a potential for serious risk to the health, safety, or welfare of a subject; (2) is for use in supporting or sustaining human life and represents a potential for serious risk to the health, safety, or welfare of a subject; (3) is for a use of substantial importance in diagnosing, curing, mitigating, or treating disease or otherwise preventing impairment of human health and presents a potential for serious risk to the health, safety, or welfare of a subject; or (4) otherwise presents a potential for serious risk to a subject.

Sponsor
A sponsor is a person or other entity that initiates but does not actually conduct the investigation. An entity other than an individual (e.g., a corporation or an agency) which uses one or more of its own employees to conduct an investigation that it has initiated is considered to be a sponsor, not a sponsor-investigator, and the employees are considered to be investigators. The sponsor of an investigational device must be located in the United States (see 21 CFR 812.18).

Sponsor-investigator
A sponsor-investigator is an individual who both initiates and actually conducts, alone or with others, a clinical investigation, i.e., under whose immediate direction the investigational device is administered, dispensed, or used. The term does not, for example, include a corporation or agency. The obligations of a sponsor-investigator include those of an investigator and those of a sponsor.

Subject
A subject is a human who participates in an investigation, either as an individual on whom or on whose specimen an investigational device is used or who participates as a control. A subject may be in normal health or may have a medical condition or disease.

Transitional device
Transitional device is a device subject to section 520(l) of the FD&C Act and which FDA previously regulated before May 28, 1976.

Unanticipated adverse device effect
Unanticipated adverse device effect is any serious adverse effect on health or safety; any life-threatening problem or death caused by, or associated with a device, if that effect, problem, or death was not previously identified in nature, severity, or degree of incidence in the application; or any other unanticipated serious problem associated with a device that relates to the rights, safety, or welfare of subjects.

Premarket Approval (PMA) – 21 CFR Part 814

Premarket approval (PMA) is the FDA process of scientific and regulatory review to evaluate the safety and effectiveness of Class III medical devices. Class III devices are those that support or sustain human life, are of substantial importance in preventing impairment of human health, or which present a potential, unreasonable risk of illness or injury. Due to the level of risk associated with Class III devices, FDA has determined that general and special controls alone are insufficient to assure the safety and effectiveness of class III devices. Therefore, these devices require a premarket approval (PMA) application under section 515 of the FD&C Act in order to obtain marketing clearance. Please note that some Class III pre-amendment devices may require a Class III 510(k).

PMA is the most stringent type of device marketing application required by FDA. The applicant must receive FDA approval of its PMA application prior to marketing the device. PMA approval is based on a determination by FDA that the PMA contains sufficient valid scientific evidence to assure that the device is safe and effective for its intended use(s). An approved PMA is, in effect, a private license granting the applicant (or owner) permission to market the device. The PMA owner, however, can authorize use of its data by another.

The PMA applicant is usually the person who owns the rights, or otherwise has authorized access, to the data and other information to be submitted in support of FDA approval. This person may be an individual, partnership, corporation, association, scientific or academic establishment, government agency or organizational unit, or other legal entity. The applicant is often the inventor/developer and ultimately the manufacturer.

FDA regulations provide 180 days to review the PMA and make a determination. In reality, the review time is normally longer. Before approving or denying a PMA, the appropriate FDA advisory committee may review the PMA at a public meeting and provide FDA with the committee's recommendation on whether FDA should approve the submission. After FDA notifies the applicant that the PMA has been approved or denied, a notice is published on the Internet (1) announcing the data on which the decision is based, and (2) providing interested persons an opportunity to petition FDA within 30 days for reconsideration of the decision.

The regulation governing premarket approval is located in Title 21 Code of Federal Regulations (CFR) Part 814, Premarket Approval. A class III device that fails to meet PMA requirements is considered to be adulterated under section 501(f) of the FD&C Act and cannot be marketed.

Premarket Notification [510(k)]
Each person who wants to market Class I, II, and some III devices intended for human use in the U.S. must submit a 510(k) to FDA at least 90 days before marketing unless the device is exempt from 510(k) requirements. There is no 510(k) form but instead a format for the submission described in 21 CFR 807 and in the pages that follow.

A 510(k) is a premarketing submission made to FDA to demonstrate that the device to be marketed is as safe and effective, that is, substantially equivalent (SE), to a legally marketed device that is not subject to premarket approval (PMA). Applicants must compare their 510(k) device to one or more similar devices currently on the U.S. market and make and support their substantial equivalency claims. A legally marketed device is a device that was legally marketed prior to May 28, 1976 (pre-amendments device), or a device which has been reclassified from Class III to Class II or I, a device which has been found to be substantially equivalent to such a device through the 510(k) process, or one established through Evaluation of Automatic Class III Definition. The legally marketed device(s) to which equivalence is drawn is known as the "predicate" device(s).

Applicants must submit descriptive data and, when necessary, performance data to establish that their device is SE to a predicate device. Again, the data in a 510(k) is to show comparability, that is, substantial equivalency (SE) of a new device to a predicate device.

Substantial Equivalence

Unlike PMA, which requires demonstration of reasonable safety and effectiveness, 510(k) requires demonstration of substantial equivalence. SE means that the new device is as safe and effective as the predicate device(s).

A device is SE if, in comparison to a predicate device, it has…

- The same intended use as the predicate device; **and**
- The same technological characteristics as the predicate device; **or**
- Different technological characteristics, that do not raise new questions of safety and effectiveness, and the sponsor demonstrates that the device is as safe and effective as the legally marketed device.

A claim of substantial equivalence does not mean the new and predicate devices must be identical. Substantial equivalence is established with respect to intended use, design, energy used or delivered, materials, performance, safety, effectiveness, labeling, biocompatibility, standards, and other applicable characteristics.

Until the applicant receives an order declaring a device SE, it may not proceed to market the device. Once the device is determined to be SE, it can then be marketed in the U.S. If FDA determines that a device is **not** SE, the applicant may resubmit another 510(k) with new data, file a reclassification petition, or submit a premarket approval application (PMA). The SE determination is usually made within 90 days and is made based on the information submitted by the applicant.

Abbreviated 510(k)

Over the past few years, FDA has been placing greater emphasis on the development of guidance documents to communicate regulatory and scientific expectations to industry. In the 510(k) area, numerous guidance documents exist, while others are under development for Class I, Class II and pre-amendments Class III devices. With the advent of Good Guidance Practices, device-specific guidance documents are developed with public participation. The main focus of these guidance documents is the identification of the information recognized as appropriate for marketing authorization. FDA believes that use of these device-specific guidances may provide an effective means of streamlining the review of 510(k)s through a reliance on a "summary report" outlining adherence to relevant guidance documents. A 510(k) submission that conforms to an FDA guidance document should be easier to prepare and review, thus resulting in a more expeditious evaluation and clearance of the 510(k).

The SMDA introduced the concept of special controls as a means by which the safety and effectiveness of Class II devices can be assured. Special controls are defined in section 513(a)(1)(B) of the Act as those controls, such as performance standards, post-market surveillance, patient registries, development and dissemination of guidelines, recommendations, and other appropriate actions that provide reasonable assurance of the device's safety and effectiveness. As in the case of guidance documents, summary information that describes how a special control(s) has been used to address a specific risk or issue should reduce the time and effort to prepare and review 510(k)s.

In addition to device-specific guidance documents (hereinafter referred to as guidance documents) and special controls, CDRH is committed to recognizing individual consensus standards. In fact, the Modernization Act amended section 514 of the Act to specifically authorize the Agency to recognize all or part of national and international standards through publication of a notice in the Federal Register. Recognized standards could be cited in guidance documents or individual policy statements, or established as special controls that address specific risks associated with a type of device. IEC 60601-1 is an example of such a consensus standard. It has broad applicability to many electromedical devices. FDA's recognition of this standard, combined with modified review procedures, should streamline the review of many 510(k)s for devices covered by the standard. Finally, by using accompanying particular standards to adapt a general standard to a specific device, the 510(k) review process may be further expedited.

Therefore, device manufacturers may choose to submit an Abbreviated 510(k) when: (1) a guidance document exists, (2) a special control has been established, or (3) FDA has recognized a relevant consensus standard. An Abbreviated 510(k) submission must include the required elements identified in 21 CFR 807.87. In addition, manufacturers submitting an Abbreviated 510(k) that relies on a guidance document and/or special control(s) should include a summary report that describes how the guidance document and/or special control(s) were used during device development and testing.

In an Abbreviated 510(k), a manufacturer will also have the option of using a third party to assess conformance with the recognized standard. Under this scenario, the third party will perform a conformance assessment to the standard for the device manufacturer and should provide the manufacturer with a statement to this effect. Like a Special 510(k), the marketing application should include a declaration of conformity signed by the manufacturer, while the statement from the third party should be maintained in the DMR pursuant to the Quality System Regulation. Responsibility for conformance with the recognized standard, however, rests with the manufacturer, not the third party.

The incentive for manufacturers to elect to provide summary reports on the use of guidance documents and/or special controls or declarations of conformity to recognized standards will be an expedited review of their submissions. While abbreviated submissions will compete with traditional 510(k) submissions, it is anticipated that their review will be more efficient than that of traditional submissions, which tend to be data intensive. In addition, by allowing ODE reviewers to rely on a manufacturer's summary report on the use of a guidance document and/or special controls and declarations of conformity with recognized standards, review resources can be directed at more complicated issues and thus should expedite the process.

Investigational Device Exemption (IDE):
An investigational device exemption (IDE) allows the investigational device to be used in a clinical study in order to collect safety and effectiveness data required to support a Premarket Approval (PMA) application or a Premarket Notification [510(k)] submission to FDA. Clinical studies are most often conducted to support a PMA. Only a small percentage of 510(k)'s require clinical data to support the application. Investigational use also includes clinical evaluation of certain modifications or new intended uses of legally marketed devices. All clinical evaluations of investigational devices, unless exempt, must have an approved IDE before the study is initiated.

Clinical evaluation of devices that have not been cleared for marketing requires...

- An IDE approved by an institutional review board (IRB). If the study involves a significant risk device, the IDE must also be approved by FDA;
- Informed consent from all patients;
- Labeling for investigational use only;
- Monitoring of the study and;
- Required records and reports.

An approved IDE permits a device to be shipped lawfully for the purpose of conducting investigations of the device without complying with other requirements of the Food, Drug, and Cosmetic Act (Act) that would apply to devices in commercial distribution. Sponsors need not submit a PMA or Premarket Notification 510(k), register their establishment, or list the device while the device is under investigation. Sponsors of IDEs are also exempt from the Quality System (QS) Regulation except for the requirements for design control.

Review Question: What does the following statement refer to? "FDA believes that use of device-specific guidances may provide an effective means of streamlining the review of 510(k)s through a reliance on a summary report outlining adherence to relevant guidance documents."
a) Alienated 510(k)
b) Alleviated 510(k)
c) Abbreviated 510(k)
Answer: c

Good Clinical Practices (GCP)
Good Clinical Practices (GCP) refers to the regulations and requirements that must be complied with while conducting a clinical study. These regulations apply to the manufacturers,

sponsors, clinical investigators, institutional review boards, and the medical device. The primary regulations that govern the conduct of clinical studies are included in the Code of Federal Regulations, Title 21 (21 CFR):

- 21 CFR 812, *Investigational Device Exemptions*, covers the procedures for the conduct of clinical studies with medical devices including application, responsibilities of sponsors and investigators, labeling, records, and reports;
- 21 CFR 50, *Protection of Human Subjects*, provides the requirements and general elements of informed consent;
- 21 CFR 56, *Institutional Review Boards*, covers the procedures and responsibilities for institutional review boards (IRBs) that approve clinical investigations protocols;
- 21 CFR 54, *Financial Disclosure by Clinical Investigators*, covers the disclosure of financial compensation to clinical investigators, which is part of FDA's assessment of the reliability of the clinical data;
- 21 CFR 820 Subpart C, *Design Controls of the Quality System Regulation*, provides the requirement for procedures to control the design of the device in order to ensure that the specified design requirements are met.

In Vitro Diagnostic (IVD) Devices Definition

In vitro diagnostics are medical devices that analyze human body fluids, such as blood or urine, to provide information for the diagnosis, prevention, or treatment of a disease. The device classification for these devices can be found under 21 CFR 862, 21 CFR 864, and 21 CFR 866.

Labeling

In Vitro Diagnostic Products have special labeling requirements and distribution restrictions under 21 CFR 809, In Vitro Diagnostic Products for Human Use. Additional guidance can be found under "Device Advice Labeling Requirements for In Vitro Diagnostic Devices."

Clinical Laboratory Improvement Amendments (CLIA) of 1988
In addition to FDA regulation under the Food, Drug, and Cosmetic Act, in vitro diagnostic (IVD) devices are also subject to the Clinical Laboratory Improvement Amendments (CLIA) of 1988. This law established quality standards for laboratory testing and an accreditation program for clinical laboratories. The requirements that apply vary according to the technical complexity in the testing process and risk of harm in reporting erroneous results. The regulations established three categories of testing on the basis of the complexity of the testing methodology: waived tests, tests of moderate complexity, and tests of high complexity. Laboratories performing moderate- or high-complexity testing or both must meet requirements for proficiency testing, patient test management, quality control, quality assurance, and personnel. These specific requirements do not apply to tests in the waived category.

In January 2000, the categorization of commercially marketed in vitro diagnostic tests under CLIA was transferred from the Center for Disease Control and Prevention (CDC) to FDA. CDRH's Office of In Vitro Diagnostic Device Evaluation and Safety (OIVD) determines the appropriate complexity categories for clinical laboratory devices as they evaluate premarket submissions. Waived products, devices exempt from premarket notification, and devices under premarket review by other FDA Centers are also processed by OIVD. Responsibilities currently assigned to CDC, including review of test systems, assays, or examinations not commercially marketed as IVD products, remain with CDC.

The Center for Biologics Evaluation and Research (CBER) has expertise in blood, blood products, and cellular therapies as well as the integral association of certain medical devices with these biological products. To utilize this expertise, CBER reviews marketing and investigational device submissions (Premarket Notification, Premarket Approval, and Investigational Device Exemption) for medical devices associated with the blood collection and processing procedures as well as those associated with cellular therapies. Although CBER reviews these products, the medical device laws and regulations still apply.

The Center for Devices and Radiological Health (CDRH) has implemented a Third Party Review Program. This program provides an option to manufacturers of certain devices of submitting their 510(k) to private parties (Recognized Third Parties) identified by FDA for review instead of submitting directly to CDRH.

The Safe Medical Device Act (SMDA) requires that hospital and other health care providers report to the FDA or equipment manufacturer when they think a medical device has or may have caused or contributed to the death or serious injury of a patient. Most hospitals have a Risk Management person responsible for coordinating all reporting under SMDA. You will need to know who that person is at each of your accounts.

If a medical equipment-related incident occurs, the healthcare provider must…

- Minimize harm to the patient
- Provide medical attention
- Notify the physician
- Notify the department head, who will notify Risk Management

- Impound equipment – save all disposable material and packaging and do NOT change the settings
- Obtain the Equipment Incident Kit from an AMMA cart or designated location
- Complete an occurrence report

As a medical sales representative, you must report any incidents where your equipment and or implants may have been involved. You may be required to offer information during a Risk Management investigation. You will need detailed notes, and may need to collect any devices and return them to your manufacturer for analysis. In such circumstances, the manufacturer must keep the devices, and Risk Management will request a report.

<u>Review Question:</u> As a medical sales representative, you must report any incidents in which your equipment and or implants may have been involved. True or false?
<u>Answer:</u> True

<u>Establishment Registration</u>

Establishments involved in the production and distribution of medical devices intended for marketing or leasing (commercial distribution) in the United States (U.S.) are required to register with the FDA. This process is known as initial establishment registration. Registration provides FDA with the location of medical device manufacturing facilities and importers. No registration fee is required. An establishment means any place of business under one management at one physical location at which a device is manufactured, assembled, or otherwise processed for commercial distribution. The "owner/operator" of the establishment is responsible for registration.
Owner/operator means the corporation, subsidiary, affiliated

company, partnership, or proprietor directly responsible for the activities of the registering establishment.

Registration of an establishment is not an approval of the establishment or its devices by FDA. That is, it does not provide FDA clearance to market. Unless exempt, premarketing clearance is required before a device can be placed into commercial distribution in the U.S.

The regulation for registration can be found in Title 21 Code of Federal Regulations, Part 807.

Most medical device establishments required to register with FDA must list the devices they have in commercial distribution including devices produced exclusively for export. This process is known as medical device listing and is a means of keeping FDA advised of the generic category(s) of devices an establishment is marketing. Each generic category is represented by a separate classification regulation found in Title 21 Code of Federal Regulations Parts 862-892 or FDA assigned device name. Each regulation number or device name is associated with one or more product codes. Regulation numbers with more than one product code identifies the product in further detail. For example, "Manual Surgical Instruments for General Use," 21 CFR 878.4800, contains several product codes including GAB (disposable suturing needle), GDX (scalpel), HTD (forceps) and HRQ (hemostat).

The Center for Biologics Evaluation and Research (CBER) currently regulates under 21 CFR Part 1270 human tissue intended for transplantation that is recovered, processed, stored, or distributed by methods that do not change tissue function or characteristics and that is not currently regulated as a human drug, biological product, or medical device. Examples of such tissues are bone, skin, corneas, ligament, and tendon. Part 1270 requires tissue establishments to screen and test donors, to prepare and follow written procedures for the prevention of the spread of communicable disease, and to maintain records.

FDA is in the process of revising the regulation of human tissues, cells, and cellular and tissue-based products. The proposed regulatory approach would address a broader scope of products, include more comprehensive requirements to prevent the transmission of communicable disease, and would apply tiered requirements based on the characteristics of such products.

CBER does not regulate vascularized human organ transplants such as kidney, liver, heart, lung, or pancreas. The federal Health Resources Services Administration (HRSA) provides oversight and funding support for the nation's organ procurement allocation and transplantation system, coordinates national organ and tissue donation activities, funds research to learn more about what works to increase donation, and administers the national bone marrow registry program.

CBER also regulates xenotransplantation, which is any procedure that involves the transplantation, implantation, or infusion into a human recipient of either (A.) live cells, tissues, or organs from a nonhuman animal source or (B.) human body fluids, cells, tissues, or organs that have had ex vivo contact with live nonhuman animal cells, tissues, or organs. Xenotransplantation using cells and tissues has been used experimentally to treat certain diseases such as neurodegenerative disorders, liver failure, and diabetes, where human materials are not usually available.

Review Question: Which of the following is NOT a human transplantation tissue regulated by CBER?

a) Bone
b) Skin
c) Corneas
d) Leather
e) Tendon

Answer: d

Electronic Human Cell and Tissue Establishment Registration (eHCTERS)

On January 19, 2001, the Food and Drug Administration published a final rule that requires human cells, tissue, and cellular and tissue-based product establishments to register with the agency and list their human cells, tissues, and cellular and tissue-based products (HCT/Ps) The final rule, 21 CFR Part 1271, became effective on April 4, 2001 for human tissues intended for transplantation that are regulated under section 361 of the PHS Act and part 1270. It will become effective for all other HCT/Ps when the remaining parts of 21 CFR Part 1271 are finalized.

As explained in 1271.21, establishments covered by the final rule must register within 5 days after beginning operations. An annual update is required in December and changes in HCT/P listing within 6 months of the change. If the ownership or location of the establishment changes, an amendment to the establishment registration must be submitted within 5 days of the change.

13. HIPAA Basics for Industry Representatives

The following section is not intended to replace HIPAA training requirements, and every medical sales representative requires a complete course in HIPAA with respect to the Final Rule and Privacy Rule (45 CFR Part 160 and 164).

The Health Insurance Portability and Accountability Act of 1996, Public Law 104-191, was enacted on August 21, 1996. Sections 261 through 264 of HIPAA require the Secretary of the Department of Health and Human Services to publicize standards for the electronic exchange, privacy, and security of health information. Collectively these are known as the *Administrative Simplification* provisions. HIPAA required the Secretary of HHS to issue privacy regulations governing individually identifiable health information, if Congress did not enact privacy legislation within three years of the passage of HIPAA. Because Congress did not enact privacy legislation, HHS developed a proposed rule and released it for public comment on November 3, 1999. The final regulation, the Privacy Rule, was published on December 28, 2000 (65 FR 82462). The final modifications were published in final form on August 14, 2002 (67 FR 53182). The final rule can be found at 45 CFR Part 160 and Part 164

HIPAA includes provisions designed to encourage electronic transactions and also required new safeguards to protect the security and confidentiality of health information. HIPAA protects patients' medical records and other health information provided to health plans, doctors, hospitals, and other health care providers. In addition to protecting the information and maintaining confidentiality the regulations also provide patients with access to their medical records, and gives them more control over how their information is used and disclosed.

The Health Insurance Portability and Accountability Act of 1996 protects health insurance coverage for workers and their families when they change or lose their jobs.

The Administrative Simplification provisions of HIPAA require the HHS to establish national standards for electronic health care transactions and national identifiers for providers, health plans, and employers. It also addresses security and privacy of health data.

HIPAA COMPLIANCE – PRIVACY RULE

The privacy regulations ensure a national floor of privacy protections for patients by limiting the ways that health plans, pharmacies, hospitals, and other covered entities can use patients' personal medical information. Medical records and other individually identifiable health information contained on paper, in computers, or communicated orally is protected health information. The privacy rule encompasses oral, written, and electronic information. The Office of Civil Rights (OCR) implements and enforces the Privacy Rule. The Privacy Rule includes provisions for use and disclosure of protected health information. Where state privacy laws are more stringent than HIPAA's privacy rule, the State Law will continue to be enforced.

Marketing is any communication about a product or service that encourages recipients to purchase or use the product or service. Marketing is also an arrangement between a covered entity (CE) and any other entity whereby the covered entity discloses protected healthcare information (PHI) in exchange for direct or indirect remuneration, for the other entity to communicate about its products or services encouraging the use or purchase of those products or services. A covered entity must obtain an authorization to use or disclose PHI for marketing except face-to-face marketing communications between a CE and an individual, and for a CE's provision of promotional gifts of nominal value. An authorization for marketing that involves the CE's receipt of direct or indirect remuneration from a third party must reveal that fact. Pharmacies, health plans, and other covered entities must obtain authorization prior to disclosing PHI for marketing purposes. Doctors, pharmacists, and other healthcare providers are permitted to communicate freely with patients about treatment options and other health-related information including disease-management programs and treatment options

Workforce members generally include employees, volunteers, and trainees. Workforce members may also include other persons whose conduct is under direct control of the entity whether or not they are paid by the entity. The CE must have and apply appropriate sanctions against workforce members who violate its privacy policies and procedures or the Privacy Rule. A CE must mitigate any harmful effects it learns was caused by use or disclosure of PHI by its workforce or its Business Associates in violation of its privacy policies and procedures or the Privacy Rule

A CE must maintain reasonable and appropriate administrative, technical, and physical safeguards to prevent intentional or unintentional use or disclosure of PHI in violation of the Privacy Rule. These safeguards must limit incidental use and disclosure pursuant to otherwise permitted or required use or disclosure. Safeguards might include shredding documents containing PHI prior to disposal, securing medical records with lock and key or pass code, and limiting access to keys or pass codes.

A CE may not require an individual to waive any right under the Privacy Rule as a condition for obtaining treatment, payment, and enrollment or benefits eligibility. A CE may not retaliate against a person for exercising rights provided by the Privacy Rule, for assisting in an investigation by HHS or another authority, of for opposing an act of practice that the person believes in good faith violates the Privacy Rule.

For internal uses, a CE must develop and implement policies and procedures that restrict access and uses of PHI based on the specific roles of the members of their workforce. These policies must identify the persons, or classes of persons, in the workforce who need access to PHI to carry out their duties, and the categories of PHI to which access is needed, and any conditions under which they will need the information to do their jobs.

Covered Entities must ensure that all business associates agree to adhere to their privacy procedures as well as to HIPAA in its entirety. Business Associate Contracts are required and serve to limit liability on the part of the CE. The agreement must establish the permitted and required uses and disclosures of PHI. A CE may disclose PHI to a BA and may allow a BA to create or receive PHI on its behalf if the CE obtains satisfactory assurance that the BA will safeguard the information.

HIPAA Civil and Criminal Penalties

Congress provided penalties for covered entities that misuse personal health information. For civil violations, OCR may impose monetary penalties up to $100 per violation, up to $25,000 per year for each requirement or prohibition violated. Criminal penalties can range from up to $50,000 and one year in prison for certain offenses; up to $100,0000 and up to five years in prison if the offences are committed under false pretenses. If the offenses are committed with the intent to sell, transfer, or use PHI for commercial advantage, personal gain or malicious harm, the penalties may include up to $250,000 and up to 10 years in prison

The health care provider may be held responsible for training sales representatives as part of their workforce. When in the O.R. observing a procedure, a device representative might be considered a health care provider.

Discussion of patient medical information is limited to work or patient care discussions and must take place in private areas. Public discussions such as in elevators, cafeterias, etc. are strictly prohibited. Never discuss the patient history, radiological exams, procedural information or any other patient specific information with anyone other than the surgical team or company as necessary for the procedure. Never hold any such discussion about a patient in a public area, and when and where you do hold such a discussion, ensure that no unauthorized persons are able to hear your discussion. On the phone, request confirmation from the other party that no unauthorized persons may be listening, and avoid the use of speakerphones. Inappropriate discussion by individuals and/or discussion in inappropriate locations will be monitored and will not be tolerated Any unnecessary discussion of patient information will result in the reprcsentative being denied access to the account, and potentially facing civil or criminal penalties as per HIPAA guidelines.

Sales representatives should not at any time view the O.R. schedule. All scheduling information is to be obtained from the surgeon's office and/or the charge nurse or advanced clinician. In the O.R. or other department or medical office, never review or record patient names or confidential information without prior authorization. Should the surgeon's office provide a patient name, the representative is to refuse to take the name, but rather only the time, date, and details of the procedure. Invoices should include the patient's medical record number or account number as assigned by the provider and obtained from the circulating nurse, the date and time of the surgery, and the name of the surgeon.

In certain situations, a covered health care provider may disclose PHI to a medical device company without the patient's written consent only if the medical device company is a health care provider as defined by the Rule. A medical device company meets the Privacy Rule's definition of "health care provider" if it furnishes, bills, or is paid for "health care" in the normal course of business. "Health care" under the Rule means care, services or supplies related to the health of an individual. Thus, a device manufacturer is a health care provider under the Privacy Rule if it needs protected health information to counsel a surgeon, determine the appropriate size or type of prosthesis for the surgeon to use during a patient's surgery, or otherwise assist the doctor in adjusting a device for a particular patient. Similarly, when a device company needs protected health information to provide support and guidance to a patient, or to a doctor with respect to a particular patient regarding the proper use or insertion of the device, it is providing "health care" and, therefore, is a health care provider when engaged in these services.

Enter the surgical suite or procedure room only after the patient is prepped and draped unless otherwise requested by the circulating nurse or surgeon. Leave immediately upon completion of the use of your product, with the confirmation from the surgeon and surgical team that the rep's presence is no longer required. The circulating nurse as patient advocate may refuse admittance to any company representative if the surgeon has not obtained written consent from the patient to have the representative present for the procedure. Suppliers are limited to the surgical suite and the procedure to which they are assigned by the physician/surgeon. (Outside the O.R., suppliers are limited to the departments where they have a scheduled appointment.)

Use of cameras in the O.R. is strictly prohibited unless written consent has been given by the patient and provided to the advanced clinician prior to the start of the procedure. Cellular phones with cameras are not to be utilized within the hospital or medical offices.

Review Question: Discussions about patients may be held in a public area under the condition that only hospital staff are present. True or false?
Answer: False. You still have to keep information away from staff not involved in that patient's care.

Review Question: Which of the following is NOT a HIPAA approved privacy safeguard?
a) Closing documents in an unlocked file cabinet
b) Shredding documents prior to disposal
c) Securing medical records with lock and key or pass code
d) Limiting access to keys or pass codes
Answer: a.

14. Sexual Harassment and the Sales Representative

All institutions will have a policy regarding sexual harassment.

Harassment is unprofessional, inappropriate behavior. There are two types of sexual harassment:

Quid pro quo is a Latin term meaning "this for that," and refers to sexual harassment involving threats or rewards. Typically, an employee is threatened with the following for failing to go along with someone's sexual advances:

a) Loss of his or her job
b) A blocked promotion
c) Demotion
d) Transfer
e) Poor job performance evaluation

Rewards for accommodating sexual advances could include:

a) Promotions
b) Raises
c) Job training opportunities
d) Continued employment

The harasser does not have to be the victim's direct supervisor.

The most common kind of sexual harassment is called "hostile environment." This occurs when a co-worker, supervisor or anyone else with whom the employee comes into contact on the job creates an abusive work environment, or interferes with the employee's work performance because of the victim's gender. Several offensive acts or offensive conduct creates a hostile work environment. These may include sexual pictures, calendars, graffiti or sexual objects, regular use of offensive language, jokes, gestures or comments.

Anyone may be considered a harasser if that person's behavior towards another person becomes unwanted, offensive, hostile or creates an offensive and disruptive work environment. You cannot assume that your behavior is acceptable to everyone with whom you come in contact. What is acceptable behavior to some people is NOT always acceptable behavior to others. Whether harassment is intended or unintended, you may be appropriately accused of harassment if you carry out any of the following actions:

- Making sexual comments about a person's clothing or body
- Telling sexual jokes or using sexual innuendoes
- Touching, hugging, patting or kissing
- Displaying offensive pictures or objects
- Using lewd or offensive gestures

Be aware of how people respond to what you do and say. If an individual objects to your behavior towards him or her, apologize and listen to the person's objections. Regardless of your intention, it is how you are perceived that counts.

Review Question: It is only considered harassment when the harasser is the direct supervisor of the victim. True or false?
Answer: False

15. Professionalism and The Business of Building Trust

The representative, who sincerely takes the consultative approach, providing truthful, reliable information about the product and its indications, will build a relationship of trust. The truth about sales is that regardless of industry, the sales representative is in the business of building trust. Representatives that successfully build trust and are sincerely being a consultant to the institution on a consistent basis will build an identity of professionalism that will result in loyalty and partnership.

The fastest way to make the sale is not always the best way to retain business long term. Taking a consultative approach to gain information on customer needs prior to recommending product will allow for a greater chance of the product being prescribed for the most appropriate indications. Having product used for fewer and more appropriate indications will produce greater outcomes, and result in respect for the representative and the company as a competent and reliable consultant.

Competence, reliability, sincerity, and consultant—what do these behaviors look like?

- What words are spoken?
- What body language is observed?
- What actions are taken?
- What responses are generated?

How your customer perceives you is a direct result of your words, listening ability, body language, and the actions you take or fail to take. Sincerity is key in building trust. To demonstrate sincerity in your communication, be sure that your words and actions are consistent and in alignment. If you talk about the importance of being on time, do not be late. If you tend to hold others (co-workers, friends, etc.) accountable to a certain standard, hold yourself to the same or to a higher standard.

Walk your walk and talk your talk every moment of every day. And do not think for one second that this will be easy! The fact that this is difficult gives you the opportunity to set yourself apart from your competitive representatives.

During a consultative conversation, you must listen very carefully and very sincerely, allowing yourself to truly understand the comment or request. Before responding, think about your response and what it may imply for the customer. If necessary, clarify the customer's statement or question prior to responding.

The better you know your customer professionally, the greater the impact you can have during a communication. As you respond to a comment or request, you will want to consider the professional history of the customer, what motivates the customer to make a purchase or recommend a product, what his or her evaluation criteria might be, etc. Take responsibility both for your understanding, and for your customers understanding of any communication.

Do you ever notice as you listen to someone speak, or even as you speak, that there may be a multitude of thoughts spinning through your mind? You may be thinking about your next appointment, the phone call you forgot to make before this meeting, what you need to do to prepare for dinner tonight. The possibilities are endless. Become aware of these thoughts, and as much as possible, when you are listening to your customer, focus on the customer's words, and prevent your mind from wandering. Maintaining eye contact is a great way to remain focused on the conversation. Planning ahead helps as well—if you are on time, have allowed sufficient time before your next appointment, and are generally well organized; your mind will be less likely to wander. Consider also, that your customer likely has a multitude of thoughts in his or her mind. A truly powerful communicator listens for both the words and thoughts and responds accordingly. Remain focused and attentive, making eye contact and interacting with the customer through your expressions and gestures, as well as your verbal communication, and you will have very productive communications.

When you are listening or speaking, your unspoken thoughts show up in your body language and facial expression. People are very perceptive, and will notice if your body language and expression are not consistent with your verbal communication. Incongruence here may appear as a lack of sincerity.

Know your product and the competitor's product—this is the basis upon which you build your sales strategy. You will need to take all the investigational information you have collected, and tie it in with your knowledge of both your own product and the competitive options. As you consult with your customer, determine the indications for which your product can truly be advantageous to the patient, and relay that information.
By being a true consultant with your focus on benefiting the patient, rather than being driven to meet sales numbers, you will create a lasting and unshakable relationship.

Anyone can learn tactics for selling against the competitions weaknesses, but when you focus on meeting the needs of specific patients for specific indications, you set yourself apart and develop trust and integrity in the customer's eyes.

16. Customer Management

In the hospital pharmacy, the selling cycle for a new product may be significantly longer than selling to a non-institutional pharmacy. This is predominantly due to the formulary process and the role of the Pharmaceutical and Therapeutics (P&T) Committee. Several persons in a variety of positions need to be included in the process of selling to an institution utilizing a formulary system. The representative will need to lobby the pharmacist and the P & T committee, in addition to the physicians. At most hospitals, the physicians will need to make applications to add new medications to the formulary. Some hospitals may allow the Pharmaceutical Company to submit applications via the Pharmacist or other members of the P&T Committee, and may allow the company to make presentations to the P&T Committee. This is a much more complex sale than just selling to a physician in private practice.

The selling cycle for a new medical device may be very lengthy. Factors that will lengthen the selling cycle include:

- New technology that requires a capital purchase
- New technology that replaces existing equipment or implants owned by the account
- Technology that is developing so quickly that it may become obsolete in a short period of time
- New technology that requires a change in surgical technique
- Complicated instrumentation
- Implants or instruments that have many pieces and/or require assembly on the surgical field
- Technologies from a new or little known manufacturer
- Accounts with existing research agreements or established loyalties
- Accounts where previous representation from your company was not well received

Several persons in a variety of positions need to be included in the process of selling medical devices to be used in a hospital or operating room. The representative will need to meet with the appropriate surgeons, materials managers and purchasing executives, as well as nurses, scrub techs and sterilization staff.

The following illustration demonstrates the cycle:

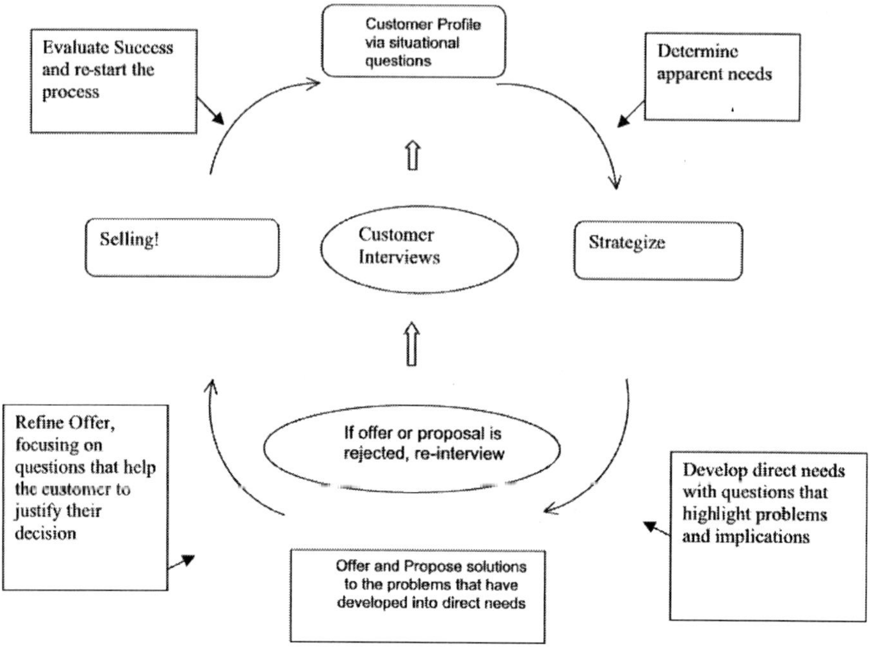

The interview process is the starting point upon which the entire selling cycle is based. Your first contact is usually with the appropriate physician. In some hospitals, it is necessary to clear any products through the Materials Management Department or Surgery Department prior to promoting the products to the physicians and surgeons. It is well advised to contact the Operating Room Manager or Director, or the Materials Management or Purchasing Departments prior to presenting any product to the physicians and surgeons. One of the aforementioned will be able to inform you of the hospital's policies and procedures for medical sales representatives so that you may prevent any mistakes that will be costly in the long term. Ultimately, you will want to meet with all doctors, appropriate charge nurses, and all other decision makers and influencers. Hospital policies may limit whom you may meet with. During your consultative questioning with the doctors and materials management departments, ask questions to determine who is involved in the decision making process at that account, and meet with as many of these people as possible. You will find differences in the purchasing motivations and evaluation criteria of each individual. You will find those who wish to champion your product, those who are indifferent, and those who want to veto your efforts. As you meet with each person involved in the process, determine the needs, and note any specific individual preferences, buying habits or motivations.

The interview process is the starting point and the basis upon which the entire selling cycle is based. Your first contact as a pharmaceutical sales rep is the Pharmacy department, where the head of pharmacy will give you an overview of the hospital specific formulary system, and will let you know what the policies and procedures are with respect to adding new medications to the formulary. When selling in the formulary system, it is crucial to determine who is on the P&T Committee.

As you come to understand more and more about each individual's preferences and habits, your sales strategies will become more successful. As your questions work to deepen the understanding of the customers' needs (both you and the customer will achieve a better understanding here), and you can make offers and proposals that will directly answer those needs, you will find morc and more members of the buying center transforming into champions of you and your products.

As a consultant, you will only be of value in offering service if you can determine the needs of your customer, and your customer's customer. This requires questioning techniques that lead to the development of a customer profile. Once you understand your customer, and the needs and motivations, then

you can strategize as to how best to bring your products and services in alignment with the needs of the hospital.
Who is the customer's customer? The obvious answer is the patient. Additionally, any person or group affected by the patient outcomes or by the business affairs AND anyone with authority over patient outcomes or financial affairs is the customer's customer. Specialized associations from whom hospitals and medical professionals would like to gain recognition are those such as the American College of Surgeons, the Association of PeriOperative Registered Nurses, and The American Society of Health-System Pharmacist. The list is extensive. Within the hospital any group that has control over your customer, is that customer's customer, such as the Credentialing Committee, the P& T Committee and the Administration.

It is also important to recognize your customer's family as the customer's customer. Occasionally, an advancement in treatment may result in improved outcomes to such an extent, that the physician received fewer calls late at night, fewer consults with the ER or decreased procedure time resulting in more efficient use of time spent at work. All of these circumstances can result in improvements in the physician's personal life. An example of this was the approval of Bone Morphogenetic Protein to replace bone graft in certain spinal surgeries. This decreased the operative time by 45 minutes for most surgeons.

Situational Questions are questions to gain factual and logistical information.

- Who are the decision makers?
- What are the important processes?
- Where will I find the MRI?

Although very important in creating the Customer Profile and gathering historical and background information, situational questions should be kept to a minimum. The danger here is that the customer may begin to feel time is being wasted on information that may seem trivial. Get as much of this information as possible from departmental and office support staff. And, be sure that they are enjoying the process. Starting out with a new customer by annoying his or her support staff can create a roadblock to access and success.

Questions to uncover problem areas are where you begin to delve into the conditions and symptoms patients may present with. You can ask what types of medications or procedures are being utilized and how effective they are.

- What adverse reactions have been experienced?
- What complaints do the patients have about their condition post-operatively?
- What concerns do you have about utilizing devices off-label?
- What policies does the hospital have with respect to off-label use?

As problems and needs are uncovered, you will want to develop them from small issues that the physician and patients are used to having to put up with, or have become used to dealing with, into a real issue that they need to have solved. You will want to develop the customer's needs in such a way, that your product and/or service become the best solution.

Ask questions that will make the individual think about the concerns as stated, and ask about the possible implications of not meeting those needs or addressing those concerns.
As they consider the implications of not having their needs met, and begin to realize what improvements would be experienced

if those little annoyances were no longer affecting their lives, the needs will gain significance. A small consideration can become a very urgent need as they consider the implications associated with failing to meet that need. During this process, you will be adding value to your solution, preferably before even offering the solution.

By taking the time to develop the customer's needs, and then offering solutions that match with the direct need as stated by the customer, your role as a consultant will be firmly set. Now you have achieved a level of credibility greater than most representatives will ever imagine. You are now ready to partner with the account, and build a lasting and unshakable relationship.

Special Strategies for Hospital Sales

The following are some traditional strategies utilized to develop relationships with physicians and other members of the buying center. These methods will allow you to make contact with your customers, allow you to provide them with valuable information about your products, and help to develop your identity as a resource.

Grand rounds are regularly scheduled meetings that may include speakers on particular topics of interest to the physicians of a particular specialty. Grounds Rounds may also be a time where the specialists discuss particularly difficult cases, and get advice from their peers on how to proceed with treatment. At times, they may ask advice of representatives who are present, regarding the indications or side effects of a particular product. At academic institutions, the rounds serve as a teaching event for residents and students. The residents are often given topics to present, and are asked to present and discuss cases, so that the staff physicians can question and critique the residents. Each area of specialization may hold weekly or monthly rounds.

In the city of San Diego, the orthopedic and neurosurgeons have organized "City Wide Spine Rounds." Each month, a guest speaker is invited to give a lecture, and, after the lecture, cases are presented and reviewed by the surgeons and residents in attendance. Each month, a different company sponsors the meeting, and the company often recommends a speaker who champions their product. Similar events are held in various cities and institutions, and by different specializations.
At Grand Rounds, nurses, pain management specialists, therapists, and other related healthcare professionals often attend regularly in order to learn more about the patients they are helping to treat. Sales representatives may often attend, in order to learn more about the patients being treated with their products, and occasionally they may sponsor the rounds.

You may find a great way to get some quality time with a physician is by providing lunch for the office. When providing lunch, it is important for regulatory reasons to ensure that you are in attendance, and that you provide educational materials at the same time.

Most physicians will make themselves available to even a new rep for a period of several minutes if the representative has provided lunch for the office. This is most likely one of the best initial strategies for a new rep, as well as for an established rep.

One may organize talks where a speaker – usually a physician consultant for the medical company – is brought in to give a talk to a group of physicians and other healthcare professionals. The representative may be present, and will generally have a table set up in the back of the room with samples, literature and snacks, as well as a sign-in sheet in order to be eligible for continuing education credits.

If you have a product or technology that is new or innovative, it may be possible to organize a presentation for a group of interested decision makers. Presentations are particularly important when selling capital equipment, as the large purchases tend to be made by committees, and long trials and evaluations are generally organized that include presentations as a part of the bidding process.

Some hospitals have regular drug and product fairs where all pharmaceutical and medical companies are invited to set up a small booth. Physicians and other hospital staff can come by to ask questions or get information about specific products. This setting allows for a lot of contact with the representatives.

You may be able to get authorization to make a presentation to the P&T Committee. As a sales representative, there may be a Product Specialist or Institutional Sales Specialist to make this presentation for you. You may even be able to have a Physician Consultant under contract with your pharmaceutical company make this presentation. Product knowledge will be key to the success of this presentation. You will need to know the science behind your product as well as other/competitive drugs of the same class. You will have to make a case for both patient benefits and financial implications of utilizing the medication.

Physicians and surgeons are scientists, and often like to get involved in the research and development of new treatment options. Research-oriented doctors are usually found working in teaching hospitals, or hospitals that have an association with a college or university. Some doctors in private practice and not associated with a college or university, are still interested in taking part in clinical trials, and they often have high patient volumes that are conducive to clinical trials. As you get to know your doctors, find out what their level of interest is in research and/or clinical trials. Involving a doctor in these activities is a great way to develop a partnership relationship and gain additional new business.

A physician consultant agreement may go hand in hand with a research project. However, there are often opportunities for doctors to have a consulting agreement independent of any specific research agreement. Doctors as consultants may be called upon to work on research projects, to speak at company sponsored meetings and educational events, or to give advice on product design. Physician consultants often develop loyalties that result in additional business for the company. Additionally, by nature of the relationship, the physician will be exposed to both new and existing products at an educational event, resulting in increased sales.

An example one of the authors experienced was inviting a surgeon using a competitive product to teach a course for young surgeons on specific surgical techniques utilizing our company's instrumentation. The result was a conversion of 50% of his business to our instrumentation, because of one key instrument that caught his attention during the course.

For Pharmaceuticals: Selling to the Pharmacy Department

The pharmacy department is your first stop in the hospital. The director of Pharmacy can provide very important information to ensure that your future business in the hospital progresses smoothly. The pharmacy department will inform you of the policies and procedures you will need to follow. There may be some specifics that were not in the vendor packet you received when you signed in. The pharmacy knows who prescribes what, and what related departments or administrators will be of value to you in building your sales strategy. They can often provide detailed information about each physician that will help you to determine how your product will fit into the physician's practice prior to your first meeting. This is crucial, as physicians are unlikely to give a new rep much opportunity or time to make a good first impression. Most physicians will only give you significant time once you have established a relationship with them.

It is important to note that the Pharmacist is usually very knowledgeable about available medications. It is a good idea to ask if the pharmacist is familiar with a product before you start educating him or her about it. Even if the product was only just released, they may have been following literature and research regarding the product for some time.

Sample questions for a first meeting with the Pharmacist:

- Could you tell me about the process in this particular hospital's pharmacy for introducing a new medication to the Formulary?
- What role does the hospital administration play in process of adding a product to the formulary?
- Who, other than yourself (by title), is involved in the process, and what roles do they play?
- What can I do as a sales representative, to assist or expedite this process?
- Who else do you recommend I speak to with regard to promoting the advantages of my product, and why it should be added to the formulary?
- May I have a copy of your form for making an addition to the formulary at this hospital?

- Once a request for an addition has been submitted, what steps must occur in order for it to be approved?
- Under what circumstances might that process be expedited, and how would that occur?
- What evaluation criteria does the P&T Committee consider when reviewing a new product application?

On a follow-up visit you may want to ask some specific questions regarding any activity from physicians relating to your sales efforts with the physicians:
"Has Dr. Smith prescribed any of my products?"
"Do you know if he/she applied to have Product X added to the formulary?"

The second visit is a good time to go into product detail. Ask,
"How familiar are you with Product X?"
"What side effects have you encountered with it?"
"Would you like some additional information on it?

Once you have an existing relationship with the Pharmacist, and your products are on the formulary, you will want to consult with the pharmacist regarding the products' performance and the doctors' prescribing habits. Ensure that the products are being prescribed for the correct indications, and if concerns arise, go back to the physician to learn why the physician chose to use the product in a manner other than what was recommended. The physician may have believed that it would be effective for an off-label indication, or it may have been a mistake. Be very careful not to jump to the conclusion that the prescription was made in error, but rather take the approach of curiosity. Learn from the pharmacist and physician how and why decisions are made.

<u>Selling to Physicians and Specialists</u>

In selling to physicians and specialists, it is important to know your product and its applications. You will want to call on the appropriate physician for the appropriate product. At times the physician who prescribes a particular drug may surprise you. For example, it may be surprising to some that a cardiac surgeon's patients often suffer from sleep disorders due to a fear of never waking.

Physicians may see 5 to 10 representatives a day, and with hectic patient loads, will not have more than a few seconds for each representative. It is important to have samples and information in your hands, and get right to the point when the doctor is able to give you a moment of his or her time. If you do not know your product the first time you make contact, you will be less likely to be given a second opportunity. It is very important to be professional, polite, and respectful. If the physician is obviously busy, leave some literature and samples and come back another time.

Persistence pays off. Most physicians like to see a representative every other week--assuming you have product that fits in with their practice. Although the physicians may not take the time to speak with you on each visit, they will want you to ensure that the office is stocked with adequate supply of samples and patient literature.

How often a physician will want to see a particular representative will depend on many factors including the following:

- How well the product fits in with their practice
- How often they perform procedures utilizing your equipment or implants
- How experienced they are with your products

- How often your company produces new devices
- How well they like you

The most important aspect may very well be how well the physician and his or her staff like you. You will need to demonstrate a very high level of respect for each member of the physician's office team, both in person and on the phone.

Some offices will require you to set an appointment with the nurse or receptionist, while others may simply tell you to drop by unannounced. Private practice physicians are more likely to have a drop-in policy than those with offices inside a hospital. It is best to make appointments with physicians and specialists through their offices. Some doctors may prefer being contacted in outpatient clinics, the operating room between cases, the fracture clinic between patients, or at grand rounds. For the most part, it is not a good idea to sell during grand rounds, unless you have sponsored that day's rounds as an educational event.

The purpose of the initial meeting is to make that person want to see you again. You want to build the identity of Professional Consultant right away. Demonstrate the ability to listen and give the impression that you are there to fulfill the physicians' needs, and to be of service. You may only have a few brief seconds to give one or two sentences about your product and why they might be interested in it. Sometimes you will be limited to leaving some samples and literature. If time allows, get into a discussion about a particular condition, and how the physician prefers to treat it. If you are given a set appointment, you will know how much time you have.

Some times you may be given 10 minutes or more, in which case you may want to ask two or three brief informational questions regarding the practice and patients seen, and main categories of conditions treated as follows:

- "Hi Dr. Smith. I am the new representative for First to Market Medical Knick Knacks. Do you mind if I ask you a few questions about how I can best be of service to you and your patients?"
- "What are your expectations of a sales representative, and what qualities do you prefer a representative have?"
- "Of all the representatives who call on you, you must have a favorite. What is it about that person that you really like? Is there anything about that person you would change if you could?"
- "Tell me about your patients. What are the most common conditions you are treating? What percent of your practice is represented by each of these categories?"
- "What percentage of your patients present with ____________ (condition or symptom)?"

So far these have mostly been situational questions. You need to move quickly in to questions to uncover needs that your product may address. If you researched your customer, and know your product, this should flow easily.

- "For your patients experiencing requiring spinal fusion, what are their most common post-operative complaints?"
- "How would an implant system that eliminates the need for harvesting bone graft be of value to you or any of your patients?"

Most often, you will be dropping in and waiting for a few seconds with the physician or nurse practitioner. In this situation you must be brief and to the point. It the product you are selling is new or unique, you will want to open with a quick statement to that effect, and that may get you some additional time with the physician.

It may take a few visits before you get an opportunity to have even a brief conversation. Be persistent, courteous, and professional, and eventually you will have an opportunity to get into more detail.

The more time you have, the more detail you want to uncover. If time allows, you may use a sequence of questions like the following:

- "Dr. Smith, for your patients requiring an ACL repair, what is your preferred technique? What do you like about that particular surgery? How could the procedure be improved? What is your opinion on bio-resorbable screws?"
- "What do you like about that particular treatment?"
- "How could the product be improved upon?"
- "Are there any conditions for which you have not found a treatment you prefer? What qualities would you prefer in a medication for that condition?"
- "Hi Dr. Smith. I was wondering if you had had an opportunity to use Device X?" If the response was "yes", then ask how satisfied both the doctor and the patient were with the results. If the doctor does not intend to reuse, you need to find out why. If in that scenario the doctor had not yet prescribed it, you might ask, "Under what circumstances would you consider using it?" Perhaps it cannot be used, as the hospital does not stock it. The representative might then ask, "What would need to occur to get it in the hospital's stock?"
- A well-prepared representative will do a trial close by asking, "Dr. Smith, the O.R. Committee is meeting next week to review new devices. Can I count on you to ensure that product X is reviewed and approved at next weeks meeting?"

At the end of the meeting, you want to request a new appointment to discuss a product in greater detail, or to follow-up on the physician's decision to prescribe your product. If there truly is no match between the physician and what you sell, do not waste his/her or your time. Thank the doctor for seeing you, inform him that you don't believe your product matches his practice, and offer to return when you have something that may be beneficial. You may still provide the doctor literature on what you have, in the event that he may find a need for it.

Always make sure you close the meeting with a question that will deliver you to the next level. At times the next level may simply gain a commitment to meet again and continue the discussion. Other times, you will make a true close where you ask for an order. In medical sales, a trial close may sound like this:

"Dr. Smith, you stated that you would like to try the new device. What patient do you have booked for surgery right now, that you would like to utilize the device for?" The surgeon may have a name in mind, or may need to look at the schedule to see what is booked. Continue getting the details including the date and time, O.R. contact person, and all logistics of completing the surgery with your company's device.

What differentiates between a trial close and a final close? The customer's response is truly what makes the difference. When you believe you have a commitment, it is time to do a trial close. Only when you ask the closing question, will you know if the commitment is real. Too often representatives will leave believing they have a commitment with details still to be ironed out. That sale is NOT closed. Only when all details are worked out and the agreement signed (or at least verbally defined and sealed with a handshake) have you truly closed the sale.

Once you have an established relationship, you will be able to ask more detailed questions, and delve deeper into the physician's mindset. Your questioning will now be much more conversational and informal. The physician's primary customer is the patient, and you want to ensure that the patients' needs are met through the use of your products.

An additional role as a representative is to provide clinical follow-up and feedback to the company, to assist them in researching, developing and improving products. When you have an established relationship with a physician, they will appreciate your being active in this important consulting activity.

Each department will be organized differently within the hospital, but will have similarities in the hierarchy of the personnel. Your job is to utilize a few situational questions to determine the key players in each department, and what role they may play in the formulary system—if any! There are some departments that meeting with may simply not represent an effective use of your time or theirs.

In the ER, you will want to meet with key physicians and nurse practitioners, as well as the department manager or coordinator. For the physicians working in the ER, this may be the only place you are ablc to contact them to request a meeting. Keep in mind that the ER can be a very busy and stressful work environment. Recognize when the ER is busy, versus when there may be some down time. If the department is busy, offer to reschedule your appointment.

Respiratory therapists, although not able to prescribe medication, may be influential in decisions regarding patient medications. It may be worthwhile to meet with the department manager, and offer to provide information on medications for COPD, asthma and other respiratory related conditions.

Radiology and Interventional Radiology and Interventional Cardiology departments may be of value depending on the products you are selling. There are pharmaceutical products specific to these areas that would require meeting with the radiologists, interventional radiologists, interventional cardiologists or radio pharmacists. These professionals may not have offices outside their respective departments. As you question physicians and specialists in their offices, you will determine the need to address these departments.

The Operating Room or Surgery Department is similar to the ER, in that it can be very hectic. The operating room is also a place where sterility and security are exceptionally high. As such, it is a location where you should avoid booking appointments if at all possible. The pharmaceutical representative will not likely need to visit the operating room. Likewise for Labor and Delivery, the Nursery, and the ICU, NICU and PACU. If you discover that there are key contacts in these departments—perhaps personnel on the Credentialing Committee or the P & T Committee, make appointments to meet outside the department if possible.

<u>Review Question:</u> What might be a negative consequence of asking problem questions (choose all that apply)?
a) The physician may become frustrated that it takes too long to get a new device on the formulary
b) The physician may be annoyed that the problems you are uncovering are too trivial
c) The physician may become agitated if you touch on a sensitive topic

d) You may reveal a problem better addressed by a competitive product

Answer: b, c, d - any of these may occur. You will need to consider your questions in such a way that you can prevent these situations or reactions, and have a plan of addressing these situations if they do occur.

17. Powerful Acts of Communication

The next four items are communication actions or tools that an excellent communicator will learn how to utilize to communicate effectively, and in doing so produce a very professional identity.

A declaration brings a thought into existence. Those who hear the declaration perceive the declared thought as "real." They may agree, disagree or be otherwise moved by the statement to produce new thoughts, declarations, etc. Ultimately, the declaration of a thought is what creates opportunity for action.

In sales, making an offer generally creates a basis for negotiation or exchange of products or services. An offer is often a promise to provide a product or service. A powerful offer answers an already defined need of the customer or the customer's customer. An offer, to be effective, should be stated in measurable terms. Consistently fulfilling offers and promises will produce an identity of reliability, and in doing so build trust.

A request is the counterpart to an offer. In sales, a request also tends to create a basis for negotiation or exchange. Requests made by sales representatives need to specify measurable parameters. The sales representative who fulfills requests promptly, accurately and consistently will develop an identity of reliability and competency, and in doing so build trust.

What happens when you are unable to fulfill an offer or request as agreed upon? Regardless of circumstance or responsibility, it is imperative that the representative in this situation apologize for failing to fulfill the obligation. With an apology, it is best to make a new offer. Very often, not wanting to look bad, the representative makes the mistake of offering excuses or rationalizing the situation, rather than simply apologizing. Once you have apologized, extenuating circumstances may be communicated in order to maintain credibility. This is particularly true if circumstances truly were beyond your control. Unfortunately, if you have not first apologized, any explanation will not likely be heard.

It is extremely important that an apology be offered prior to the deadline with respect to fulfilling an obligation. If it looks like there may be a delay or setback, apologize and offer a new deadline in advance of the expiration of the original deadline. Failure to negotiate new terms PRIOR to the deadline will weaken the apology and reduce your credibility.

18. Selling at the executive level

In today's hospital market with HMOs and contractual supplier agreements, it is very tempting to sell directly to hospital executives. Although there may be situations where this becomes appropriate, in order to get to this level, all influencers en route must be kept informed, as they will have veto power. In order to gain respect and cooperation to allow for a high probability of a sale, with few or no roadblocks along the way, the best strategy is to start at the bottom, and include all appropriate personnel on the way up the ladder.

By making all influencers and decision makers a part of the process, you will have the ability to not only gain their agreement, you will have them assist you in getting to the executive level, and this will pave the way for a true business partnership.

It used to be that the doctor simply informed the hospital of what he wanted to use, and the products were purchased by the hospital for the doctor's use. Those days have ended at 99.9% of the hospitals across America! However, the doctor does want it to appear as easy as that.

Nurses, sterilization staff, and materials and O.R. managers are far more involved in the decision making process than ever before. In order to gain their respect and cooperation and to allow for the sale to complete, with few or no roadblocks along the way, the best strategy is to start at the bottom and include all appropriate personnel on the way up the ladder. By making all influencers and decision makers a part of the process, you will have the ability to gain their agreement and have them assist you in getting to the executive level.

This thorough process paves the way for a true business partnership. By partnering with the hospital in this manner, the doctor is kept happy, as the doctor is prevented from hearing complaints from other members of the buying center regarding the process of acquiring the instrumentation that he or she wishes to utilize.

It is crucial that the representative adheres to policies and procedures set out by the hospital. One cannot say enough about the importance of demonstrating respect for all hospital staff at all times. This means everyone from the parking attendant to the CEO. Your behavior within the facility is constantly being monitored. An example of the downfall of one rep's identity and respect was when he was seen driving disrespectfully as he cut off an ambulance when he was running late for an appointment at the hospital. Several years later, he still pays for a mistake he made prior to even entering the facility.

The most important component of your long-term success in hospital selling is also the one over which you have the most control. It is your day-to-day commitment to providing exceptional customer service.

19. Resources

Other UniversityOfHealthCare CDs and books with more information on the topics covered and related topics:

- Agent GCP and the Bloody Consent Form
- Agent GXP FDA Part 11
- Global Pharmaceuticals in the 21st Century
- Healthcare Fraud and Abuse Introduction
- HIPAA Focused Training 1 Overview
- HIPAA Focused Training 2 Business Associates and Covered Entities
- HIPAA Focused Training 3A Privacy Uses and Disclosures
- HIPAA Focused Training 3B Psychotherapy and Country Doctors
- HIPAA Focused Training 3C Marketing
- HIPAA Focused Training 3D Notice of Privacy Practices
- HIPAA Focused Training 4A Data and Computer Security
- HIPAA Privacy Compliance Planning
- HIPAA Privacy Certificate Program
- HIPAA Regulatory Documents
- Laugh and Learn Pharmaceutical Sales Code
- Medication Errors

- Multidrug Resistant Tuberculosis
- OSHA Bloodborne Pathogens
- OSHA Eye Safety
- OSHA Fire Safety
- OSHA Medical Radiation Safety
- OSHA Regulatory Documents
- OSHA Safe Lifting
- Pharmaceutical Regulatory Documents
- Quality Assurance and Outcomes Introduction

Other UniversityOfHealthCare sales CDs and books on sales topics:

- Advanced Sales Skills Certificate Program
- Internet Searches
- Laugh and Learn Sales Letters 1
- Laugh and Learn Sales Territory Management
- Laugh and Learn Sales Time Management
- Pharmaceutical Computer Validation Introduction
- Sales Body Language
- Sales Humor Delivery Skills 1
- Sales Humor Writing Skills 1
- Secrets of a Leadership Coach
- Writing Clearly

References

American Society of Health-System Pharmacists (www.ashp.org)
Association of periOperative Registered Nurses (www:aorn.org)
Society of Interventional Radiology (www.sirweb.org)
American Medical Association (www.ama-assn.org)
American College of Surgeons (www.facs.org)
The Medical Center of Aurora Health Care Industry Representative Protocol, February 11, 2002 (Sexual Harassment Policy)

Rackham, Neil, The Spin Selling Fieldbook, (New York: McGraw-Hill, 1996
Centers for Medicare and Medicaid Services (www.cms.hhs.gov/hipaa/hipaa2)
Department of Health and Human Services (www.hhs.gov)
Unknown, Supplier Orientation Packet (San Diego: Sharp Metropolitan Medical Campus, 2003)
Power Speaking Seminars, Leadership In Life (Toronto: Warr & Associates, 2001
Tanzer, Herb The Line (San Diego: Herb Tanzer Seminars, 2003)
Dr. Daniel Farb, Laugh and Learn Pharmaceutical Sales Code (Los Angeles: UniversityOfHealthCare, 2004)
American Medical Association (www.ama-assn.org)
American College of Surgeons - www.facs.org
American Association of Tissue Banks, Standards For Tissue Banking, (McLean:AATB, 10th Edition, 2002)
Centers for Disease Control and Prevention -
http://www.cdc.gov/ncidod/hip/Aresist/mrsafaq.htm
http://www.cdc.gov/ncidod/hip/
http://www.cdc.gov/nchstp/tb/faqs/qa.htm
U.S. Department of Labor Occupational Safety and Health Administration:
http://www.osha.gov/SLTC/etools/hospital/clinical/radiology/radiology.html#Radiation
Code of Federal Regulations - 21 CFR 812.1, 21 CFR 812.3
Goodman, Jesse L. Centers for Biologics Evaluation and Research. "Tissue Banks: The Dangers of Tainted Tissues and the Need for Federal Regulation" (Statement before the Committee on Governmental Affairs - United States Senate, May 2003)
AdvaMed http://www.advamed.org/publicdocs/code_of_ethics.pdf